PENGUIN BUSINESS

THE MILLENNIAL LEADER

Vivek Iyyani is a globally recognized leadership expert and keynote speaker, helping organizations and leaders work better together in the new normal. Vivek has spoken worldwide, to organizations and enterprises from Fortune 500 companies to associations to government institutions. He is the founder and CEO of Millennial Minds—a company that has helped leaders and teams leverage twenty-first century collaboration skills globally. He has been invited to many international media outlets to share his opinions as a thought leader on the Millennial generation. Some of his recent features include *Channel NewsAsia, Money FM, Straits Times, SME Entrepreneur Magazine, CEO Magazine,* and *National Integration Council* (Singapore Prime Minister's Office). He has authored two other books entitled *Empowering Millennials* and *Engaging Millennials*. Learn more at https://www.vivekiyyani.com and follow him at @vivekiyyani on LinkedIn, Facebook, Instagram, TikTok and Twitter.

Scan QR code to get your
bonus resources

Advance Praise for *The Millennial Leader*

Books about Millennials are always about how difficult to manage they are. Not this one! This book is more for Millennials than about Millennials. Not about how to manage Millennials, but rather how do Millennials manage? Or more accurately, how should a Millennial lead people? It is chock full of practical advice and exercises to make Millennial managers think about their roles as leaders and how to get better at it in a very different world than the one their predecessors grew up in. They are having to learn new management approaches on the fly, as there were no guidebooks for how to manage the new workforce.

Vivek Iyyani demonstrates, once again, his research abilities and his deep knowledge of Millennials. This is a practical guidebook for the new generation of leaders, well worth studying and, as Vivek suggests, using the tools to study your own leadership style. Whether you are a new leader, or an experienced leader tasked with managing the new workforce of today and tomorrow, you will benefit from reading, and re-reading, this latest book by the expert on Millennial management.

—Fermin Diez, Deputy CEO and Group Director,
National Council of Social Services

Following his very insightful book on the minds of the Millennials, Vivek has followed up with another great book on how we can proactively prepare this exciting generation of talents to become our future leaders.

—Tham Chien Ping,
People, Culture and Sustainability Director,
WhiteCoat Global

The book explores how and why the new hallmark of Millennial leadership will be risk management, autonomous management style while continuing to apply digital pivots, human behaviour &

psychology for creating value for the organization. The book will find a favourite place in the reading nook of anyone who is part of the multi-generational, high-performance teams and leaders.

—Suganya Jagannathan,
Global People Experience Director, Johnson & Johnson

Indeed, the rules of engagement has changed and should change as we head towards a multigenerational workforce. As most of our experiences and knowledge were acquired in a post-pandemic world, the importance of unlearning and relearning should take center stage. Vivek has in his own style, articulated and reinforced what Singapore's founding father, Mr Lee has said, 'I do not yet know of a man who became a leader as a result of having undergone a leadership course'. This book is a refreshing read as it provides a point of view and touches on the need to lead with a collaborative and empathetic lens, the 'human touch' as he calls it.

—Alvin Aloysius Goh, Executive Director,
Singapore Human Resources Institute

If you are an aspiring leader looking to manage more effectively in a post-COVID 19 world, I would definitely recommend reading *The Millennial Leader*. Vivek takes a candid approach towards what makes effective leadership today and makes it more relevant for readers with his personal experiences.

—Gary Lee, Global Head of OD, Bybit

Newly promoted managers may find the transition difficult to make if they are not well prepared for leadership. Packed with valuable, hands-on industry experience from Asia's leading voice on managing Millennials, *The Millennial Leader* provides a guiding light to help you avoid the painful trials and errors that plague new managers, so you can become the inspiring leader you were meant to be. A must-read!

—Marc Wong, Career Services
and Industry Engagement Professional

This is a very insightful book on the mindset of a Millennials, their motivations, preferences and thinking process in the current environment. It's applicable, and an easy read.

—Zubaidah Binte Osman (Zuby),
Head of Centre for Excellence (Distribution L&D),
Great Eastern Life Singapore

The book is brilliant and insightful. It gives a great idea on how one should tackle generations of workers and productivity in the pandemic. It not only helps us understand the challenges that Millennials face, it allows us to learn how to tackle them easily and confidently as well. It is a great book, a must read.

—Sulbha Rai, Chief People Officer, RenewBuy.com

It has been a while since I read a book that really got me thinking. Vivek delivered a holistic perspective of the challenges faced by Millennial leaders in today's work environment—the new normal. Anyone in HR and leadership roles should read this!

—Stella Sim C. P., APAC HR Leader,
Global Technology Company

I highly recommend *The Millennial Leaders* to any Millennial who desire to understand their own conflicts with attaining and sustaining their leadership journey. Vivek has clearly laid a path with clarity and understanding to those genuinely desiring an ascent in their Millennial potential!

—Kapish Gya, People Operations Associate, Rogers Capital

Vivek hits the nail on the head with *The Millennial Leader: Working Across Generations in the New Normal.* We have entered into the an era that demands a major shift in leadership paradigm where hierarchy gives way to a network of relationships. The pandemic has taught leaders a valuable lesson: embracing change is not a choice if we intend to stay in the game. Vivek's insights speak with me; they resonate with my real encounters with leaders of all generations. This book provides practical tips on what it takes to be a leader in the new normal.

—Cindy Aw, Human Resource Director,
Durapower Holdings Pte Ltd

Vivek Iyyani's new book *The Millenial Leader* is a must read for leaders with or without titles, looking to lead, make a difference, and advance. The book is extremely relevant today as the workplace has undergone dynamic changes like never before. Clearly, the definition of leadership has changed and *The Millenial Leader* probes deep into what has changed, what makes a Millennial leader distinct from any other generation, and lays down strategies to effectively lead in the new normal. The well-researched information presented in this book is the not only a solution to current workplace challenges but also the best anti-dote to half-baked and unsubstantiated information that pervades social media.

—Dr. Lakshmi Ramachandran, Learning
and Development Specialist,
National University of Singapore

I used to often wonder what is the big deal of the Millennials? Workplaces always had different generations working together. When I went through the book, I had couple of insights. Earlier days, leaders grew in the organization, gradually and picked up leadership and people management skills along the way. Also, WFA/WFH has made this more difficult. Due to rapid changes in business environment, leaders need to be more agile and adapt to changes quickly. I found this quite interesting from the book, there is no time to learn from one's own mistakes, one has to learn from others' mistakes!

The book has a very practical approach, with links worksheets for exercises and for self-evaluation as a 5G leader.

—Georgie Antony, Director, Hono

If you are making waves and leading in the workplace today, then this book is a must-read. Leading today is vastly different from what it was in the past, and your best bet to doing well is to have a clear view of the wider trends. Undeniable, inevitable and revolutionary, Vivek's insights and deep understanding of what it means to lead as a Millennial leader will set you apart from the rest.

—Yeo Chuen Chuen, Forbes Coaches Council,
Managing Director, ACESENCE
Agile Leadership Coaching and Training

A thought leader in the field of managing and engaging Millennials, Vivek has encapsulated the challenges that Millennial leaders will encounter when dealing with intergenerational teams. Offering many practical tips and actions in his latest book, this is a must read for all Millennial leaders who want to develop deeper human skills and get up to speed with the needs of today's intergenerational teams.

—Melvin Lee, City Manager, Le Wagon Singapore

The Millennial Leader is a brilliant and timely book. Vivek Iyyani offers a great deal of insights into the opportunities and challenges faced by the organizational leaders in unprecedented times. It is never more important for the leaders of the day to recognize the necessity of unlearning and relearning the meaning of leadership in order to adapt to the changing world around us. Full of powerful stories, research data, and incisive inquiries, this book is a must read for people leaders across all levels of the organization.

—Vivien Li (she/her) | Director, Human Resources,
Danaher Corporation

This is a MUST read for all Millennials, leaders or not, especially in the post-COVID era, where the norms may no longer be the norms. The future of work requires a different approach in terms of managing our 'career portfolio', and this book got it covered. What I like best about this book is not only the insights shared by Vivek, coupled with his experiences, but also the thought provoking questions throughout the book. Get your coffee ready, and it's time for a good read!

—Traven Teng, Talent Acquisition Lead, Tencent

The Millenial Leader is a very interesting book bringing together the 'old' leadership world and the new generation. I particularly appreciate the concept of moving the needle and the identification that organizations need to hold their managers accountable on DEI. In addition, for someone coming from a western company, the awareness on the Asian way of looking at topics such as burnout and Great Resignation is very insightful and valuable to support our leaders in the organization.

—Romain Lefaix, Head of HR APAC, SCOR

The Millennial Leader presents a fresh perspective on the need to shift leadership from compliance to connection. Young, aspiring leaders will benefit significantly from the insights and reflection points that this book offers—from the importance of self-awareness to the power of inclusive leadership. Seasoned professionals will also broaden their horizon in harnessing the collective talent of a multigenerationl workforce. This book challenges traditional thinking, something we need more of with the dynamic situation we face today. It is content-rich yet easy to read, set in a relatable & pragmatic tone.

—Leo Caballes, Total Rewards Director,
APAC & MEA, Electrolux

OTHER BOOKS BY THE AUTHOR

Engaging Millennials: 7 Fundamentals to Recruit, Reward & Retain the Largest Generation in the Workforce, Penguin Random House SEA, 2021

The Millennial Leader

Working across Generations in the New Normal

Vivek Iyyani

BUSINESS

An imprint of Penguin Random House

PENGUIN BUSINESS

USA | Canada | UK | Ireland | Australia
New Zealand | India | South Africa | China | Southeast Asia

Penguin Business is part of the Penguin Random House group of companies
whose addresses can be found at global.penguinrandomhouse.com

Published by Penguin Random House SEA Pte Ltd
9, Changi South Street 3, Level 08-01,
Singapore 486361

First published in Penguin Business by Penguin Random House SEA 2022

ISBN 9789814914130

Typeset in Adobe Garamond Pro by MAP Systems, Bangalore, India

www.penguin.sg

To Avighna, this one's for you

To Thoufic, who has always been there for me as a Leader

To Swathi, who taught me the value of speaking up for what you truly believe in, even if it means having difficult conversations with the ones you love and cherish

Dedicated to all the leaders of today who dare to challenge the status quo today so as to hand over a better world for the leaders of tomorrow

Contents

How to Extract the Most Value out of This Book   xv
Foreword   xix

Chapter 1: The 5G Leader   1

Chapter 2: The 7 Maxims of 5G Leadership   15

Chapter 3: 6 Challenges in the New Normal   42

Chapter 4: Why Millennials are Wired Differently   88

Chapter 5: Clarity: Leading Yourself Before You
Lead Others   104

Chapter 6: Connection: Spark and Sustain
Long Lasting Relationships   142

Chapter 7: Candor: Making Difficult Conversations Easy   166

Chapter 8: Coping Mechanisms: Dealing with Stress,
Burnout, and Overwhelm in Times
of Uncertainty   183

Chapter 9: Culture: Building an Environment
that Drives Performance   205

One Last Thing   213
Acknowledgements   215

How to Extract the Most Value
out of This Book

When I sat down to write this book, I knew that writing a book on leadership for the generation that has taken the most beating ever since they entered the workforce was important. How could it not be? The majority of the content we find about Millennials online are hating on them. Millennials killed this and that. The generation gap we experience in the workforce today widened because the world underwent a multitude of changes when the Millennials were growing up. Everything from the technological trends to the financial trends and even the sociological trends influenced the mindset that Millennials have today. Lost in the digital, artificially intelligent, volatile, uncertain, complex and ambiguous (VUCA) world of the Fourth Industrial Revolution, it isn't hard to get overwhelmed and paralyzed by the complexity of modern life.

The reality that a Traditionalist, a Baby Boomer, or Gen X experienced upon entering the workforce—including behavioural norms, management styles, what defined leadership, how people developed, and how they interacted—is different from what it is today. So are parenting styles, communication styles, and social customs. Hence, there are inevitably attitudes, ways of thinking, expectations, and modi operandi shared among those who were born, raised, entered adulthood, and joined the workforce during the same time period.

With each generation, the requirements of the leader among us have changed. Today, as Millennials enter into leadership and management roles, they are required to be the 5G leaders who leverage their tech savviness to bring people closer together.

As you read this book, I encourage you to sit in a really comfortable setting (perhaps a comfy sofa, hot chocolate, scented candles, and soothing music?) to read the book as you are about to go on an introspective journey to truly understand how many things have changed and yet, the way we still do things at work still to remain unchanged. I humbly request you to keep an open mind and heart, and lower your guard to allow for the ideas and concepts to formulate within you as you read this book.

To make the most out of this book, keep a journal next to you. Every chapter that has been written in this book has been written to force you to challenge the old and embrace the new. Each chapter contains a number of questions that you will need to reflect on, on your journey as a leader. It is in these reflections that you will gain the most insights. The more you put into the reflections, the more insights you will notice bubbling up as your mind processes the reflective questions written in each chapter. I would even recommend that you re-read each chapter because it does two things: first, it gives you better clarity of the concepts discussed and secondly, it helps you pick up ideas that you might have missed out the first time round. Reading gives you information, but it is the writing process that reveals the insights clearly.

On top of that, I've prepared a series of worksheets for different activities and exercises that come with the book. You can access those when you head over to www.vivekiyyani.com/free

As you read this book, you will realize that a lot of what you are doing is very similar to juggling. I use the word 'juggling' because it is about coping with all the different things on your plate by skillfully balancing competing things. It is a constant management of dealing with a multitude of things without letting anything drop. You might think—didn't all generations have to juggle work and life? Well, not in the same circumstances as leaders need to today. A few decades ago, work was a lot simpler. You clock in at 8 a.m. and clock out at 5 p.m. and work ends for the day. News happened from 9.30 p.m. to 10 p.m.

and that was the news of the day. Employees you managed were all full-time staff and mostly were younger than you. There were clear boundaries back then, but today, everything is mishmashed with one another and boundaries have blurred.

Millennial leaders are finding themselves in a unique situation, having to deal with more members of the older generations with different mindsets and expectations, working under them. Add remote working into the mix and it gets even more complicated. Moreover, with the gig economy gaining more popularity, the need to inspire and incentivize the gig workers while simultaneously managing artificial intelligence and technology to make everything work can naturally lead to a sense of overwhelm. This is on top of ambiguous working hours and the constant juggle of managing your boss and team performance requirements while ensuring everything else is going smoothly at home. It's not easy, I know!

The best jugglers know how to keep their eyes on what's in their hands while anticipating what's coming up next. Your organization, your boss, and your team will constantly need you and just like juggling, you will be able to juggle more and more once you start to get the hang of it. In fact, once you get the foundation right, the more you will find yourself able to juggle more and more items with ease. It is my sincere wish that this book helps you become a better leader. This book has been written for you, to help you anticipate the unique challenges you will face as a Millennial leader and to empower you with the key strategies and techniques to juggle everything like a pro. My hope is that, as you read, it will help you identify what is holding you back and how you can bring out the best from within. As you work through the book, make sure you pause at the 'Think about it' sections to reflect, journal, and do the activities as suggested, so that you can fully apply what you pick up from this book.

To see how you currently score as a leader, head over to www. vivekiyyani.com/free to do the 5G Leader scorecard and get a customized report with immediate and actionable steps as well as key videos, worksheets, scripts, and templates to help you overcome the problems discussed in this book.

Foreword

Vivek and I first met several years ago at a dialog cum networking session for business and HR leaders. It was the sort of session that one is expected to contribute to, by sharing experiences and building on the ideas that someone else has contributed.

Vivek was one of the youngest participants in the room. And I recall him speaking passionately about the rise of the millennial generation, advocating that organisations challenge their assumptions and rethink their approach to talent management as far as this demographic was concerned.

A confluence of factors including technological advancement, globalisation, geopolitical dynamics, and evolving social structures, have resulted in seismic shifts in business models and cultural norms. The pandemic further accelerated changes in the way work gets done. And yet, leadership practices are all too often rooted in outdated paradigms.

In my work as a board director and advisor, I am privileged to have a front row seat across a range of organisations that all are grappling with the need to transform themselves to stay relevant. Invariably, the pace and effectiveness of this change process comes down to leadership.

Leaders who recognise that they need to challenge long-held assumptions and reinvent themselves are the ones who can drive the organisational and culture change that is needed to turn strategy into results. This is why Chapter 2: The 7 Maxims of 5G Leadership resonated strongly with me.

As an adjunct professor of leadership, I am passionate about helping leaders become better at their craft. I am thus constantly on the lookout for resources which I can recommend to my students, be they in their 20s or their 50s.

The Millennial Leader is not just for millennials who are moving into executive and management roles. I recommend it for all leaders who are keen to lead their teams and organisations to new heights in the new normal, and ready to become Millennial Leaders at any age.

Su-Yen Wong
Global Board Director, Professional Speaker,
Adjunct Professor of Leadership

Chapter 1: The 5G Leader

Plunging into a Pandemic

28 December 2019. The first time I chanced upon it was on social media. I had just landed back in Singapore after my trip to India, and it was amongst one of the first notifications that popped up on my Instagram feed as I switched off the airplane mode. It was news of a new virus in the city of Wuhan, China, that was spreading contagiously.

I remember casually brushing it off, thinking, 'Nothing to panic about, this is in China.' Little did I know that within a month, the World Health Organization (WHO) would declare a 'public health emergency of international concern' on 30 Jan 2020. Of course, there were other pressing matters that were worthy of mention happening around the world. It seemed like we had crash landed into the new decade with a series of unfortunate events.

It started with Australia on fire, destroying habitats of over 800 vertebrate species along with over 46 million acres burnt. Soon thereafter, the news of Prince Harry and Meghan Markle quitting the royal family made the news. Somalia declared a national emergency with the locusts swarming across East Africa. Then, we lost Kobe Bryant and his thirteen-year-old daughter to a helicopter crash. One after the other, 2020 took off on a slippery slide, and in the meantime, the coronavirus was making its rounds all over the world.

It wasn't until Tedros Adhanom, Head of World Health Organization, declared COVID-19 a pandemic on 11 March 2020, with 121,564 cases worldwide and 4,373 deaths, that people started to pay more attention to the virus. Very soon after, countries with rising infections started declaring national emergencies with new 'lockdown' protocols to curb the spread of COVID-19. For the first time in my life, I saw communities across the globe panic and stockpiling on all sorts of commodities and of all things, the least I expected, toilet paper. The fact that toilet paper has no direct or indirect means of protecting one from the virus clearly meant one thing: fear was hijacking the people at large and was spreading faster than the virus itself. And it was interfering with the very nature of getting work done by gathering together in an office.

This is the moment when the transition happened where we went from one world to the next. COVID-19 was pulling the future forward, revolutionizing the workplace, breaking up with the old normal and thrusting us into a world of chaos. The public health emergency turned into a global economic crisis. Global supply chains collapsed and the flow of people crossing borders slowed to a trickle. Every organization, large and small, local and global, public and private, was profoundly impacted. We had entered the volatile, uncertain, complex, and ambiguous world.

Leading in a Pandemic

Interestingly, the pandemic revealed a great deal about the leaders we had elected as well as their ability to lead. COVID-19 is known to be notoriously hard to control, and the involvement of political leaders is only one part of the equation when it comes to pandemic management. But some current and former world leaders have made little effort to combat outbreaks in their country. This has been seen through either downplaying the pandemic's severity, disregarding science or ignoring critical health interventions like social distancing and masks. Some leaders chose total denialism over ineffective action, which made matters worse for many. Others played the blame game against China by labeling COVID-19 as 'Kung Flu' which has also led to a nearly two-fold increase in attacks on Asians in the past year in their respective countries.

In the same vein, we have had great leaders who confronted new realities quickly and fully. Doing this would have been seen as so simple and obvious and yet, most people struggled with it. These leaders, and what makes them so great, is that they took action, not knowing if they will succeed because no one else before them has done it. This may be harder than confronting new realities, as we humans are naturally risk-averse. In making a difficult high stakes decision, it is human nature to wait for more information and try to achieve consensus while burning valuable time. Such is the nature of the world we are in today, and it is clear beyond doubt that we need leaders who are attuned to the needs of the people and the world we live in today. Many of us, myself included, kept telling ourselves that this virus situation won't last long, and we will return to status quo in a matter of months.

When a major event happens that poses an existential threat, many norms of life change, some in the short term and some in the long term. Back in 2001, almost two decades ago, 9/11 made an impact on how we live and behave. In that period of fear and panic, companies stopped allowing their people to travel. Just as those policies have since faded, the airport process that gets us into the plane has changed forever. Similarly, many of the major COVID-19 changes that we're facing today will evaporate and things will go back to the way it was without much notice. We will adopt the mindsets and postures we had before the crisis and yet, COVID-19 will alter many elements of how we work in the new normal.

COVID-19 has affected business owners, rank-and-file staff, and the many managers in between. Unlike a natural disaster like a tsunami, it has been enduring for many months on end, with no firm end date in sight. It has been pervasively disruptive as it has dramatically altered the way we live and work. Grocery suppliers were disrupted, schools took on home-based learning, and people who could work from home were required to do so by the government. COVID-19 has become an impossible to ignore virus with a 24/7 nearly all-consuming news cycle, that's almost exclusively focused on the pandemic. Despite the size, scope, and intensity of the virus, some work activities will go back to the way they were, but at the same time, there will be permanent changes which will forever alter the way we think about and behave at work.

The Rules and Roles of Leadership Have Changed

We are living in a momentous time in human history. We are possibly living in the best of times and the worst of times. This era of explosive change has exposed the built-in flaws and poor foundations on which we have been working. We are long overdue in changing the way we work, and the spread of COVID-19 has made it an urgent necessity. Employers today need their leaders to be agile, seize opportunities, take initiative, and build value for their companies. The entire concept of leadership is being redefined.

The time has come for yet another big reboot in the workplace. In times of stress, it can be tempting to fall back on familiar ways of leading, so implementing change of this magnitude needs to start with each of us. How can we reduce the feelings of pressure at work and feel uplifted instead? How can we develop a culture of self-care instead of self-sacrifice? How can we form collaborative partnerships through the different sources of stress? The good news is that so many answers to the business challenges we face today are readily available, except they remain untapped. The coming years will be marked with transformational disruption unlike anything we've seen before.

According to Klaus Schwab, founder of the World Economic Forum, we are now in the Fourth Industrial Revolution which is so complex and fast-moving, it demands a new type of leadership that empowers all citizens and organizations to invest, innovate and deliver value through mutual accountability and collaboration. The old rules of the game won't work as effectively in the world we live in anymore. And yet, we are finding ourselves in a new world today that has no manual and no rules on how to play the game well.

That's where this book will come in handy.

Why You Need to Read this Book

Leaders are Readers

We have seen the turmoil that most leaders went through when faced with a challenge they had no means of preparing ahead for. In fact, those countries that experienced the challenge of dealing with SARS were much better prepared to deal with COVID-19 than other countries that had never encountered it. It goes to show the value of experience when one encounters issues that are novel; issues that can knock us off our feet.

> *A good leader is one who learns from his mistakes.*
> *A smart leader, however, is one who learns from others' mistakes.*

That is why the saying exists—*'Leaders are Readers'*. The best way you can be a smart leader is to learn from others' mistakes. This is usually explored through books, which can take you on a journey of the ups and downs of the leader. Even with all the different types of media we have available today, from YouTube videos to TV interviews to radio talk shows and even live fireside chats at events, the only medium that can really dive in deep to the subtle issues and intricacies is books. Books have the ability to share in depth the issues faced by leaders and there is so much you can learn from such shared experiences and interesting insights. This book aims to share the macro issues that are happening around the world and then fine tune it into preparing you for the micro issues you face on the ground. Learning from the many leaders who have been interviewed from this book can lead you to reach your desired outcomes as a leader at a much faster pace.

Generational Turnover

It was knowledge of the unspoken rules—certain ways of doing things that managers expect but don't explain and that top performers do but don't realize.

—Gorick Ng, Author of *Unspoken Rules*

There is no such thing that this generation should be an extension of the previous generation. This generation should do something that the previous generation could not imagine. That is when there is a purpose to this generation, isn't it? Otherwise what's the point?
                                    —Sadhguru, Founder, Isha Yoga Center

If you sense that things are changing rather profoundly in the workplace, you're correct. What is really strange is that many of the rules that made sense a decade ago don't make sense anymore. What seemed to be the norm for several generations is suddenly becoming as outdated as going to a mall to rent out a movie. In the same vein, the concept of leadership is evolving rapidly now, as the driving force of innovation in management. Up till now, for almost three decades, things were relatively stable as the Baby Boomers (born 1946–1964) occupied the office buildings. They were so vast in numbers that they had amazing influence over distinct cultural expectations at work. Their cohort size was big enough to create a steady and stabilizing effect on the workplace. Their systems, customs, traditions, and expectations have become concrete, and the workplace has become a composition of Boomers' tastes and preferences that have solidified over time.

However, things are beginning to shift again, as Millennials (born 1980–1995) start to make up the majority of the workforce. Boomers are retiring in large numbers and there is a huge turnover happening as leadership positions get handed down. The size of the affected population multiplied at the speed at which the changeover is taking place is creating a churn like never before. This is also due to the fact that Generation X (born 1965–1979) isn't as large as the Millennial generation. In many cases, Millennial leaders are now at the helm, together with Gen X leaders, to work towards navigating the new issues that have come up since COVID-19 hit. COVID-19 has sharpened our fault lines and it is highlighting many areas at work that need to be addressed. If the different generations don't learn to work well with one another, the loss of tacit knowledge, the kind of insights that can't be found on Google, will be lost with the Baby Boomers if they don't impart it to the leaders of today.

As it stands, this pandemic has become the biggest challenge of our generation, the Millennial generation, and it has become our turn now to take the wheel in the driver's seat. Born between the 1980s to mid-1990s, the first wave Millennials (1980s) have entered leadership positions and the second wave Millennials (1990s) are entering leadership positions.

As you might have noticed already, the title of this book is '*Millennial Leaders*', and it is written bearing in mind the unique challenges, threats, capabilities, and opportunities you will have during your tenure as a leader. The challenges that you will encounter in your leadership journey will be very different from the challenges faced by leaders from the previous generations. For one, due to the generational gap between the older and younger generations in your team, you will be flummoxed with mixed signals from both groups who require varying amounts of attention and have completely unexplained expectations of you as their leader. We dive deeper into the nuances in the later chapters of this book.

Technological Advancement

There is a joke that surfaced on social media that asks the question:

Who's the leading force in your company's workplace digital transformation?

a) CEO
b) CTO
c) COVID-19

There's likely more than a grain of truth underpinning the joke. The novel coronavirus forced a 'pause' button for people and industries, as large swathes of the world's population faced quarantine conditions that resembled house arrest. The majority of offline social and economic activities were suddenly off limits. Hence, the reliance on technology literally zoomed past many leaders' comfort levels. Calendars of employees working from home became filled with back-to-back 'Zoom meetings' which has created Zoom fatigue and all other sorts of issues that we are still working around today.

The one thing that became clear during this period is that, COVID-19 has forced the hand of leaders to lean into technology instead of avoiding it. This is something that has been noticed by leaders across the globe, as the very thing they hesitated to implement during pre-pandemic days. They were forced to adopt it or risk running out of business. As a result, digitalization became one of the buzzwords as news channels started showcasing role models of companies that have adopted new norms to stay competitive. When even fishmongers in Singapore started doing Facebook Lives to sell their produce through online methods, companies realized digital transformation is not something they could postpone any further.

Technology is advancing at ridiculous speeds and changing what work could be and how it gets done. Factories are moving from human labour to automated labour, and experiencing mass productive gains. Law firms are using artificial intelligence to perform research once conducted by humans. Companies are adopting autonomous vehicles to survive without a human driver.

The issue for leaders when it comes to advancing technology will not be the technology itself but rather the danger of it becoming the bright and shiny object that leads to distraction. Leaders will need to be up to speed with technology in order to be able to differentiate between technology that slows organizations down and technology that can make organizations progress faster. Leaders of today will have to answer questions like 'What will technology mean for labour?', 'What will technology mean for the mission of the organization?' and 'To what extent do we pursue technology at the expense of our human capital?' Leaders who are not grasping the gravity of the tech boom will find themselves behind the curve. These are serious questions that are answered in this book.

Be Two Steps Ahead

And that is why I wrote this book—to serve as a guide for Millennial leaders based on the problems and challenges you will face today. Firstly, the information shared by other Millennial managers and the difficulties they encountered while transitioning into management can serve you. It will help you realize that you are not alone if you're going through the same challenges. Secondly, you will have a better inkling of what to anticipate as you make the transition into management. Just like the way you felt lost while transitioning from a college student to a candidate to a current working adult, the sense of being at a loss, whether it be a loss of freedom or a loss of familiarity, remains the same as you transition into management. As awesome as it feels to achieve the results you've always desired, you must also understand that you are leaving your comfort zone. Even for the most gifted individuals, the process of becoming a leader is an arduous, albeit rewarding, journey of continuous learning and self-development. Ask any experienced manager about the early days of being the boss and if they give you an honest answer, you will hear a tale of disorientation and overwhelming confusion. Given the significance and difficulty of taking up a leadership role for the first time, managing team members of multiple generations, it's surprising how little attention has been paid to the experiences of Millennial leaders and the challenges they face.

As the world changes at frightening speeds, we need you, as leaders of this generation, to step up and deal with the challenges that get hurled our way. As it is, there are countless books that have talked about leadership at length. Many of them have great leadership concepts as well, but the only problem is that they might not be relevant to fit into today's context. So much has changed over the past few decades in terms of social norms, technological advances, and even government policies. These factors have shaped human behaviour and have changed drastically, and it is important for leaders to acknowledge this and lead with the available resources of today. Looking back at our ancestors, they did the same thing. They had to unlearn and relearn to survive. And I believe, this is what we will also need to do to continue to have meaningful work in the digital age by doing tasks that technology cannot execute well.

My aim with this book is to prepare you for the challenges that lie ahead in order to lead your team in this pandemic. Think of this book as the Global Positioning System (GPS) for thriving in uncertain times and dealing with tremendous disruptive pressures afflicting every industry. It is meant to reinvigorate your outlook and help you produce breakthrough outcomes with your team despite the disruptions that may happen during your tenure.

As a professional who has been studying the Millennial generation for a while now, I am able to see the many ways that the leaders of this generation are able to bring about change and push for better performance by leveraging on the innate mindset, skills, and competencies we have acquired over the years. I am also aware of the blind spots, pitfalls, and drawbacks that leaders of this generation need to work on to bring out the best in the teams they lead. I dive deeper into these in Chapter 4.

Sandwiched in the Middle

I remember clearly one time when I met up with a client for coaching where he was really stressed out. He started out the session with a huge sigh. He told me about the tremendous pressure he has from the top where the company directions were set and business results needed to be achieved. At the same time, when he's back in the office, he also faced the pressures from the ground where many of his team members reported to him with all the operational and administrative issues he needed to solve. He felt like the 'filling in the sandwich', pressed from both top and bottom by the 'buns' i.e. the top management and local subordinates.

With Millennials entering the phase in their careers where they are being sandwiched by the older generations and Gen Zs that are entering the workforce amidst the chaos that COVID-19 has created, you can rest assure that there will be an immense amount of pressure from work that comes with the territory. This doesn't just apply at the workplace, it applies in the same manner at home. As Millennials are settling down and starting a family, they are also being sandwiched by their parents as well as their children, which can become a strain in the precious resources such as time, money, and health. When the pressure builds, the stress follows as well. That is why it is important for Millennial leaders to be able juggle all of the things on their plate without burning out.

In the chapters that follow, I will uncover the key competencies you will need to pick up as a leader to lead in the new normal. To begin, let's have a look into the role of the leader in an organization today.

Leaders Lend Leverage

I remember the first conversation I had with my business partner when we won the tender. It was unexpected, we were in our third year of experimenting with entrepreneurship and we both felt like we had just won the lottery. We had just beat the big boys in the training industry to win a year-long tender to manage a series of camps for our client. It was a big deal for us, taking into account our age (mid-twenties) and limited experience.

As we sat in the neighbourhood coffee shop near my block, celebrating our new win while sipping on our cup of tea, my business partner Thoufic said, 'For this project, we cannot be the ones training on the ground anymore. The scope of this project is way bigger than anything we have handled till date. We'll have too many things to take care of, so we gotta find a camp chief and a team of facilitators to run the camp while we manage everything else. It will be too much to handle everything on our own if we conduct the trainings as well'.

I nodded in agreement.

We needed a lot more manpower and planning to run the project efficiently, and in the back of my mind, I knew that as much as I enjoyed interacting with youths, I could not afford to be the facilitator on the ground. We needed to build a team and lead them to deliver our program to our client. Acquiring that tender project was my foray into a leadership role.

Similar to most leaders in organizations that get their promotion after working there for a few years, my business partner and I took the plunge into entrepreneurship without much thought. Right after graduation, we set up a private limited company and started hustling for training projects. The confidence of being a trainer in schools to deliver programs to youths was something we had built up from working in multiple companies as freelancers, while pursuing our higher studies.

Until we got the big tender project, we mostly acquired smaller projects, which meant we could manage the workload we had from acquiring the sale to delivering the project to completion. The scope of planning and preparation that went into delivering short training programs for a class of thirty was way less compared to planning overnight camps for a cohort of 300. I knew for a fact that we needed to leverage on more people in order to get more work done.

This time round, my role had changed. It was no longer to engage, educate, and entertain the participants as the camp facilitator, but rather to lead a team of trainers and ensure we achieve a common goal. It was a new role, and I was thrown into the deep end, not really knowing what I should or should not do. The experience of hiring others (camp chiefs and trainers) for our gig, briefing them, training them, and supervising them to run the project on behalf of the company opened up the possibilities for us.

When we first started out, we wore all the different hats in the business, from sales to marketing to operations and administration. The work we had to do was pretty clear: market and sell our programs to the schools and universities until we secure a client. Once we secured the client, we had to prepare the slides, print out the training materials, and deliver the project to our client successfully. It was simple when it was just the two of us.

However, once we were awarded the tender, the scope of the project increased. We needed more hands on deck. The fact that we were no longer doing the work by ourselves, but rather, with the help of a team, meant that we were in charge of a team to help us achieve a specific outcome. It also meant that we had to delegate some of the work, that we used to do, to others in the team. It was a risk with a worthy trade-off: our time. If our trainers were careless and did a bad job in engaging the youths, the business was in jeopardy. If anyone in our team didn't do their part as promised, the project gets compromised.

As entrepreneurs, our survival has always been dependent on our ability to provide training programs to our clients. What we realized with the tender project was that, having a team under us gave us leverage to scale much faster. With a team, we could sell more projects and acquire a bigger clientele. The objective remained the same—provide training programs to our market. Having a team allowed both of us to focus on selling more training programs. As leaders of the company, it was our duty to ensure our team could achieve better outcomes than the two of us put together.

Performance ≠ Leadership

Ask any manager about their early days as a boss and you will hear tales of despair and disorientation. Many are hampered by myths and misconceptions and fail to surpass the trials in this rite of passage as a leader. This is where they stumble and sabotage their careers while inflicting significant costs on their organizations. Eventually, picking up the harmful and toxic practices from the past only serves to leave a trail of disengaged employees stuck in a toxic culture, something that becomes a heavy burden for organizations to bear.

The way to identify a good leader is to track their ability to work with people in order to achieve bigger and better outcomes with their team on a consistent basis. It is about being better together. The biggest challenge leaders have in today's world is not so much revenue generation or profitability. It is about productivity through the people they lead. How can they attract the best talents and nurture them in their organizations? How can leaders get the best performance from their talents? Most importantly, how can leaders get things done without picking up the toxic practices of the past and applying it onto their team? How do we, as leaders, ensure our projects get delivered on time without developing a culture of beating people up to get results? I've seen the enemy, and it is us.

The leaders set the path forward and as new leaders, you have the power to change the way things get done in your team. If you find yourself in a top-down managed company, which worked in its time, you will realize that the top-down structure is too slow in a world where speed is the currency for success. The brainpower isn't only in the executive office. It can be found throughout the organization and leading with collaboration is far more effective than the command-and-control system. The manager–worker relationship has become more of a business partnership than supervisor–subordinate execution of ideas and strategy. Today's leaders must be more intimately involved in the details of the business as facilitators and coaches, while workers are becoming more autonomous self-leaders, creating a partnership to achieve business results. As a leader, not only do you have the potential to impact the people you lead in both positive and negative ways, but also indirectly influence their family members and friends.

The principles in this book have been tested by many Millennial leaders leading regional teams across the globe and have proven that they work. It is not difficult to become a leader who is productive and a personal favourite of many if you take the steps set out in this book, in the order they are prescribed and implement them in a high standard. If you do, you won't need to resort to the old-school toxic strategies that the leaders in the past picked up to get things done. Throughout this book, I am going to ask you to question everything you currently know about leadership and then rebuild new skills to take it on. You will become highly influential in your organization very fast. They will come to you when they face problems even when you don't hold any rank because they trust you and believe you will be able to lead them properly. Simply put, you will become the leader others turn to for help when they need it, to solve problems, and get things done.

This, I believe, is the mark of all great leaders.

If you're ready to become the Millennial leader that can lead all generations without resorting to your authority, flip over to the next page . . .

Chapter 2: The 7 Maxims of 5G Leadership

Business Leadership Rooted in the Past Won't Lead You to the Future

Simon Sinek shares a story in one of his YouTube videos about how leaders can get afraid of disruption to such an extent that they avoid pushing for change. Blockbuster was the only significant national video rental chain in America. They were known as the 800-pound gorilla that totally got destroyed when this little company called Netflix showed up. Leaders at Netflix saw the rise of the internet and its potential for streaming in the future. The technology wasn't quite there yet at that time but everybody knew it was coming. That's how they started experimenting with an entirely new business model called 'subscription'. It allowed the consumer to rent the movie DVDs and keep them as long as they wanted and send them back once they were done watching. The CEO of Blockbuster at that time went to the board to persuade them to experiment with the subscription business model. However, the board would not allow him because the company made 12 per cent of their revenues from late fees. They were so afraid to give up 12 per cent of revenues that they literally committed an act of suicide. Blockbuster doesn't exist today and Netflix is determining the future of television and movies. Most people might say that the internet put Blockbuster out of business. Absolutely not.

It was their business leadership that was rooted in the past and put them out of business. We can see this happening in companies during this covid phase as well. There are companies that are desperately clinging on to their old business models but if they're not willing to pivot in this marketplace, the marketplace will put them out of business. The key is to be agile and adapt quickly. To do that, we need to realize that what got us here today won't get us there in the future.

Even if you have never been through a bad break up in a relationship, you would be able to understand the concept of emotional baggage. According to clinical psychologist John Duffy, 'emotional baggage' is the intangible but very real emotional weight we carry due to the unresolved issues or traumas from previous relationships. Until we face these issues, we'll most likely bring our baggage into each new relationship.

The same is true for leadership.

For the past 100 years, leadership has not changed much. Most companies still offer a high percentage of decision-making power to a select few. Leaders still call the shots of what the team works on, how they work, and when and where they work. Many leaders tend to micromanage instead of inspire their people. They act as gatekeepers, rather than advocates, for career development. Many 'best practices' were created for a world that no longer exists. In the face of change, the routines that once moved you forward often become the ruts that hold you back. No practice is ever perfect. The day you stop being open to improving is the day you start stagnating. Leaders are critical to building top-notch employee experiences.

As the demographics change, so does the makeup of the workforce. There's a fundamental shift in priorities for Millennial workers—a generation that is due to make up 75 per cent of the global workforce in 2025. The Baby Boomer boss, whose leadership style is based on a 'chain of command', is getting ready to hand the reins to a new generation.

Following World War II, the average age of marriage dropped, and the number of children increased dramatically. Baby Boomers became a drastically larger generation than the Traditionalists (born 1925–1945).

Hence, they had to grow up in a world that was fundamentally small for them. In the early years of the boom, schools were overcrowded and under-resourced. Colleges didn't have enough seats and competition for jobs was intense. As a result, Baby Boomers learnt the importance of competing for resources and success. They were willing to sacrifice to build a better life for themselves, even if it meant working in a work environment that was far from ideal.

Today, the workplace itself has changed too. Individual offices gave way to open plan spaces, hot desking, and even 'telecommuting'. Employees are no longer clocking in to work at 8 a.m. They are no longer given their 'task-of-the-day' and clocking back out at 5 p.m. The modern workforce is highly mobile, with employees who demand flexibility and autonomy in their work. The traditional structure of boss/employee just simply doesn't work anymore.

Our world is changing and changing fast, from the way we eat and dress to the way we take care of our health. And yet, as the modern workplace has developed and evolved, traditional leadership styles have not. What worked for the factories in the 1900s no longer applies to today's mobile, deskless, and autonomous workforce. Traditional leadership has become outdated, with Millennials and Gen Zers rejecting traditional leadership practices.

Sticking with old-school leadership tactics may not serve you or your company well. A leader's style has an influence on a company's culture. Culture influences employee behaviours and by extension, company performance. Old-school leadership tactics may adversely affect your ability to attract and retain the best of today's savvy and dynamic employees.

Every individual brings with them a myriad of experiences and ideas that are already shaping their leadership perspective. Even if you may have only hit the leadership ranks recently, you might have led in other circumstances and also observed the good and bad management. According to Bruce Avolio, this is known as the context of leadership learning. A person's life stream is like a river that flows. It represents the events you accumulate from birth to the present that shapes how you choose to influence yourself and others around you. Learning the concept of one's life stream helps to keep leadership in a constant state of growth and evolution. It is through the process of integrating your own thinking and personality into the contents which I will be sharing with you in this book that will allow you to define your own self-concept as a leader. It is this process that will ultimately shape the framework for developing, organizing, and implementing your leadership skills.[1]

A lot of the leadership development material from the early days placed a high amount of emphasis on the follower. The goal was to teach the leader to get the follower to do what he wanted her to do. Just like how parenting styles have shifted over generations, the norms of the past no longer fit in as the norms of the present. Many of the 'disciplinary procedures' that took place in the past will be seen as abuse in the world we live in today. Over the years, I am sure you will agree with me, society has progressed overall in terms of thinking and we continue to push for progress in areas that have been left unaddressed. If you've ever heard your leader start a sentence prefaced with 'Back in my day . . .' you can safely guess that back then, they meant to highlight that situations were different. All the leadership practices and philosophies that were picked up in the past were reinforced by parenting styles that existed back then. One of the most familiar phrases that come up in discussions around parenting is 'Spare the rod and spoil the child'. It is the modern-day proverb that means if a parent refuses to discipline an unruly child, that child will grow up spoiled in many ways. He will become, in the common vernacular, a spoilt brat.

I remember in the first week of joining my high school, the first event that made an impression on me as we sat in the hall was when the discipline master brought up a few students onto the stage, inserted a book into their pants, and then proceeded to cane them in front of the entire cohort of over 500 students. It was an uncomfortable sight to watch, and yet it was seen as the norm back then. If you break the rules, you get punished according to the rules. Yet, I remember as I was growing up, corporal punishment became a topic of debate and over time, it was phased out. And I was so glad it so happened.

---

[1] Espinoza, C. 2017. *Millennials Who Manage* (1st ed.). Pearson FT Press.

Like most things in life, one of the key reasons Millennials are vastly different from the generations before them, comes down to how we were raised and what we lived through as children. Millennials were raised by Baby Boomers who had a very distinct parenting philosophy that differed from the Traditionalist generation that raised them. Baby Boomers wanted Millennials to have it better and easier than they did. They worked hard to give us the things and the opportunities they never had, and the Boomers were helped by an unprecedented time of economic growth from 1970 to 2000.

Baby Boomers were raised to fit in and keep quiet. Traditionally, the man was seen as the head of the family. The father made the major decisions without quite consulting anyone about it. The same structure was replicated in the workplace with a hierarchical pyramid of bosses and subordinates. Orders were passed down from the top to the bottom and in many organizations; this remains as the status quo. Boomers were told by their parents to 'go find a job with stability'. Anything with an iron rice bowl was considered a boon and a blessing. Working in the civil service and in multinational companies were considered ideal options to build your career.

After World War II, the best leadership training was believed to be from leaders in the army. During this period, many ex-military personnel were highly sought after for leadership positions because they could set up structures and manage large organizations. Baby Boomers were subjected to the 'command and control' style of leadership under the Traditionalists and managers seemed to carry the same approach. They were responsible to nurture or punish their team members the way a parent would. As a result, Baby Boomers have always had a strong respect for the chain of command. They believe strongly in paying the price to succeed and it often involves working longer hours and giving priority to work over family.

Historically, leaders have relied on established hierarchical structures. The higher they were, the more authority they held and the more they could do what they wanted. The system was inherently patriarchal with a strong focus on men of high social status. Except for a handful of exceptions, women were typically excluded from official leadership roles altogether. Challenging leaders back then was risky business. Most discrimination laws didn't come into effect until the 1970s. CEOs and General Managers, who run major corporations today, got into the seat of leadership when companies were still operating with century-old principles. Their standards for how they treat people and how they want to be treated are largely defined by 19th-century cultural norms. Sadly, we still see such 'dinosaur' leaders today whose leadership characteristics will disappear as they retire. As younger leaders pick up the baton, it is your opportunity as a Millennial leader to take in the best practices and replace the bad practices with a 21st century consciousness into the world of leadership.

Research shows that the old model is not effective. O.C. Tanner's 2020 Global Culture Report shows that more than half of their employees say their leader won't give up control over anything. Only a mere 26 per cent of employees feel their leader encourages collaboration and only 59 per cent believe their leader values them. In fact, 20 per cent of employees mentioned that their leader openly expresses their doubts about them regularly. The impact is disastrous with these numbers. Companies that support and maintain these traditional leadership practices with such low scores suffer in areas like employee experience, engagement, great work, and net promoter score. Moreover, they have a decrease in odds of growing revenue with increased odds of laying off employees. It's pretty clear; the old school style of leadership is neither inspiring innovation nor creating a sense of belonging in their people. Leadership needs to evolve to meet the needs of the modern workforce. Forward-thinking organizations have modern leaders who mentor and coach instead of manage, who inspire great work in their people, and who trust their people and get out of their way. Organizations with this type of leader will attract top talent, have engaged employees, and retain their best people.

Unfortunately, traditions tend to bind us and as long as new leaders feel they have to role model age-old traditions, even the new leaders will pick up and repeat the unhealthy practices of the previous generations. These myths, because they are simplistic and incomplete, lead new managers to neglect key leadership responsibilities. Here are some old-school ideologies that we need to debunk and destroy in order to lead our teams better.

The Command & Control Leadership Style
is a Practice of the Past

The military functions well using top-down positional authority. For decades, many leaders adhered to the rigid leadership style where managers gave orders, enforced inflexible policies, and didn't welcome input from their subordinates. Do what the leader says, and everything simply 'works'. This type of 'command and control' leadership took hold post World War II and is a relic of a bygone era of business. Yes, there used to be a time when the Baby Boomers took office where this strategy worked really well. Competition was high, alternative work options were low and the economy was just recovering from World War II. Baby Boomers were willing to suffer all sorts of abuse at the workplace because the thought of being fired was much scarier back then. Plus, with the high level of competition, it was all about curry favoring their bosses and getting in their good books to get promoted into a private office in the corner. Expecting people to 'follow orders or else' worked well in the industrial age when you're running a factory. In that kind of setting, you expect people to be cogs—simply do instead of think or problem solve.

In today's digital age, you cannot coerce, control, or command people to do these things. Instead, you must create the conditions that enable them. The modern workforce today no longer craves private office space anymore. They don't want to work in an organization where they must simply do as they're told, with zero input on their role and direction of the company. Command-and-control leadership worked in an age where options were scarce, where employees were expected to spend their entire careers and be rewarded with a pension. Before the internet, employees didn't have as many options to change jobs, and leaving a company in search of greener pastures was not as common. In fact, in those volatile times, people valued stability and tenure over flexibility.

Are you a leader if no one really wants to follow you? Simon Sinek, author of the book, *Leaders Eat Last*, says you're not, especially if no one is following you. Unfortunately, working in a corporate environment automatically puts you in charge of a group of 'followers'.

Your employees are forced to follow you. The question is, would they still want to follow you if they had a choice? For starters, let go of the hierarchical model of leadership. Top-down leadership used to be the way of life, but today, it is more of a side-by-side relationship. The difference with using this approach in a business setting is that your employees have a lot more expertise than a military recruit who just joined the army. Treating them like recruits who know nothing could only spell doom for you in the long term. It's an insult to the value they can bring to the table. Today's workforce will not tolerate a command-and-control approach from their leaders. Employees who feel micromanaged or strictly scrutinized by their managers feel comfortable jumping ship and finding a new job where they have more autonomy, respect, ownership, and a sense of purpose.

Have you come across this phrase?

When your boss says 'Jump', you ask, 'How high?'

It would be interesting to see what actual responses you get if you were to try this out with your team. Yes, it might seem ridiculous even to think ideologies like these still apply in today's world but you would be surprised by the number of leaders who still hold on to this expectation. They hold their experience and wisdom in high esteem and expect their subordinates to follow without questioning. In fact, this used to be the norm many decades ago and somewhere deep down in many employees' minds, they have been trained to obey authority figures and follow.

Hierarchy was a real thing and respecting it was a must. In fact, it is not difficult to find leaders today who expect you to address them by 'Sir' or formally by their name because of the rank they hold. There is an established 'chain of command' that is in place. It starts and ends at specific points, and movement up or down could only be made one link at a time. When you have matters that need to be addressed, they have to go through the chain of command. Jumping the queue by going directly to the senior management's office to share your thoughts is considered unacceptable. As organizations created the hierarchical system, they also strove to protect the ranks as they achieved it. The rank empowered the older generations to treat their subordinates in less-than-ideal ways to get the work done. The power that came with the rank also revealed an ugly side of their personalities.

The problem with using rank to run matters at the workplace is this: people respect you only for your rank, and not for the relationships you build with the team members under your care. I know of teams who have such leaders and I even had a friend who told me that there are two WhatsApp groups for his teams—one with the leader and one without. Many leaders who aren't well liked by their team aren't well respected once they leave the room. The young generation, that is generally more 'woke' and aware of the malpractices and their 'rights' at work, are not afraid to challenge malpractices by leaders in the organizations today.

I remember an incident back when I was on a road trip in India. There were six of us. We had just finished shopping on day two of our ten-day trip. I was driving, and my dear friend, who was sitting next to me, forgot to put on her seatbelt. Within 50 meters of driving, a police officer stopped us, asked her to wind down the window, and asked her why she wasn't wearing her seatbelt.

All of us felt that cold chill run down our spines as the police officer asked her to disembark from the car to settle this issue. At that moment, my brain jammed, and I was trying my best to get it to work again. I didn't know what to say, so I just went up to the police to plead for leniency. My friend was freaking out, worrying about the consequences and how this will affect the trip. She was on the brink of tears and was enveloped by tremendous guilt. The police officer sternly looked at us, then took out a piece of paper, and then wrote down Rs 5000 and asked us to cough up—as a fine for not wearing a seatbelt.

I didn't even bother trying to ask for leniency. I turned to my friends to start asking them for their share of cash to quickly pay off the fine. It didn't occur to me back then, that there is a fixed amount to offenses like this that have been published online. I was ready to chip in and pay up so that we could get on with our trip. That was my immediate response. But then, one of my other friends, Virali, the youngest amongst us, quickly pulled up her smartphone, jabbed her fingers at it really quickly, and then went up to the officer like a boss and said,

'But sir, online it shows that a fine for not wearing a seatbelt is only Rs 1000. Why are you charging us Rs 5000?'

Virali had actually navigated to the Indian government's website through her smartphone and sourced out an official document that displayed all kinds of fines for all kinds of offenses. Upon seeing that document, a senior officer, who wasn't really paying attention to us, suddenly took interest. He looked at the document as she showed it on her phone, and then did something completely unexpected. He said, 'It's okay, you kids can carry on. Don't worry, just wear your seatbelt next time.' He even 'shushed' that police officer who wanted to fine us when he objected to letting us go scot-free.

I heaved a sigh of relief. 'Thank god for the Internet,' I thought to myself. We couldn't believe it, but common sense told all of us that we should scoot from that place instantly—with seatbelts on. As we entered the car, we continued to look at each other with disbelief. Just like that, an online document that Virali accessed through a basic Google search saved us from being fined for breaking the law and also prevented the police officer from pocketing a profit of Rs 4000 from the inflated Rs 5000 fine he came up with on the spot. Virali was the star of that trip and is still hailed as a superstar today in our group for her 'boss move'.

This event really made me reflect about the behaviours we have been taught in life. Simply deferring to authority because they have a rank or a uniform does not mean they are all angels with a moral compass. If police officers who are meant to protect the law can be the very people to abuse the power and trust they hold, it is not difficult to imagine other leaders in power resorting to all sorts of malpractices to achieve their selfish desires.

The Internet and Google has definitely empowered the individual who knows when to use it. Even though I knew how to Google back then, it never occurred to me in that moment of time that a Google search could save us from being mistreated. Like my friend Virali, many employees today will seek for answers through an inter-connected community powered by the internet before they approach the people in their network.

While fundamentally Millennials don't have an issue with hierarchy, we don't see hierarchy in the same way the previous generations did. The Millennial generation is more about collaborating together as a team and prefer flat structures that create a better experience. Being part of social networks today, connections are seen as a spider web as opposed to a hierarchical chain. Therefore, obtaining a rank or a corner office doesn't really speak to the Millennials. In fact, the more informal the relationships are between the team members, the better. Millennials don't really subscribe to the idea of using rank to run things in their team.

Most new leaders, partly due to their insecurity in a new role, yearn for compliance from their subordinates. They think that if they don't establish this early on, their direct reports will climb over their heads, and as a means of gaining control, they rely a lot on their formal authority. This technique is questionable at best. Even if someone was able to achieve some measure of success through formal authority, they have achieved false victory. Compliance does not equal commitment. If people aren't committed, they won't take on initiatives. And if they don't take initiatives, the manager will not be able to delegate effectively.

The issue with the military-style management is that it sacrifices employee satisfaction for short-term results. Sacrificing employee happiness means forgoing long-term performance. Employees who are stuck under 'old-school' managers would certainly not say they have a 'great place to work'.

It would be naive to think that this style of management cannot be found in younger leaders because there will be those who 'grew up' under this style of management. People use the same style of approach as those who mentored them. There are also certain industries that use this style of management to this day which makes it hard to eradicate completely. The military style of management will not win any favour in this day and age. If you thought that you would be given special rights and privileges that come with being the boss, that you would have more freedom and autonomy to do what you think is best without being burdened by unreasonable demands from others, think again.

Yes, leaders do wield some power. The problem is that most of them mistakenly believe their power is based on the formal authority that comes with their new position. The assumption that new leaders tend to have is that adopting an autocratic approach is the most effective way to produce results. New leaders soon learn, however, that when direct reports are told to do something, they don't necessarily respond. Most leaders today are realizing painfully that the source of their power only comes from establishing credibility with their subordinates, peers, and superiors. Yes, some leaders have even expressed shock and felt insulted that their position, expertise, and track record do not count for much.

Instead of feeling free, most new managers tend to feel constrained as they get enmeshed into a web of relationships. You have to work with bosses, peers, and many other stakeholders who will make relentless and often conflicting demands on you. Being a leader in this day and age means you have to give up the myth of authority for the reality of negotiating interdependencies. Building strong and meaningful relationships with the key people that the team depends on will be a necessary skill to pick up on. The need to demonstrate competence and character is of particular importance to your team members. This, coupled with your level of influence by building strong relationships with various stakeholders, will set the foundations right in building a strong team.

Times have changed and the leadership practices that we have adopted from previous generations have to change to suit the working environment we live in today. If the only reason behind your following questionable, age-old management practices is the treatment you received from your manager in the past, then you're just a well-trained leader, not a well-educated one.

* * *

The old days of command-and-control leadership is fading in favour of what might be better termed a trust-and-track method. This is where workers are not just told what to do, but why they are doing it.

More formally, business is moving from what was called 'transactional' to 'transformative' leadership. And there's no turning back.

* * *

Don't Let Them Know Only when They Screw Up.

There's a meme that's floating around Instagram based on the movie *Shang Chi*. For a bit of background, *Shang Chi*, upon release, has been lauded as one the few movies that really portrays the Asian culture as accurately as possible. So naturally, a meme has to be made about this.

Friend: 'What's the most unrealistic part about Asians in Shang-Chi?'

Me: 'The part where the mother holds the son close to her and says, "I'm so proud of you".'

The only reason this is funny (memes are meant to be funny) is because there's an element of truth in it. Asians are not known to be very expressive with their feelings of appreciation. This applies not only at home, but also at the workplace. Parents in the East, especially Baby Boomers and Gen Xers, do not verbalize their love for their offspring as much as it is done in the West. While it does not mean that the parents love their children any less, it does highlight a flaw in how we express our acknowledgement and appreciation in the Asian culture.

Bring this back to the workplace and it was not uncommon to see bosses yelling at their team members in front of the entire team. The very leader that you respect and look up to can shake the foundation of your self-beliefs with the way they admonish their team members. Somehow, leaders have seemed to pick up a notion that appreciation of your team members will make them soft and is counter-productive to getting things done. Having such a masculine approach to leadership could be attributed to the fact that there were fewer female members in leadership positions at the management level when Baby Boomers and Gen Xers were working. It is even a commonly held belief amongst many that the females who made it to the top, had to work like a man in order to climb the corporate ladder. Being supportive, accessible, demonstrative and communicative is unfortunately not something we associate with the leaders and the relationship we hold with our bosses.

As Millennial leaders, I believe that acknowledgement and appreciation is a powerful tool that leaders can use to build a peak performance team. It makes the workplace less formidable, and much more inclusive in nature as we embrace what it means to be more human.

As a leader of team members from different generations, you will start to notice mixed signals within your team when it comes to feedback. For instance, the older generation grew up with the notion that their bosses will only give them feedback when they mess up. In other words, no feedback was good feedback. In fact, the feedback sessions back in the day used to border on the line of abuse and no one really looked forward to being called into the manager's office. Performance reviews were done on an annual basis for most older employees and it was not something they looked up to. Even till today, when your manager says, *'Can I see you in my room? I need to speak to you,'* many coaching clients of mine experience shudders of anxiety down their spine as they imagine the worst as they walk to their manager's room.

However, the younger generations grew up in a different world where all their adult figures since childhood have been reaching out to them to support them in their success. Parents took a more democratic approach in raising their children (Millennials & Gen Zs) by seeking their opinion and giving them a voice. School counselors were around to guide them to take the best path for their academic pursuits and career. The younger generation is used to getting the counsel of the adult figures around them and is known to speak up even when their opinions are not sought after.

As a Millennial leader, this might be confusing when one group doesn't really require your weekly one-to-one sessions, whereas another group is constantly seeking for affirmation for the work they've completed and feedback to make things better. That's why it is crucial that you don't take a one-size-fits-all approach to engage with your team members. Different members from different generations will have different expectations and requirements, and I'll be covering these factors in the later part of this book.

It Doesn't Have to be Lonely at the Top

The common saying amongst leaders is that 'It's lonely at the top'. As managers, you know you were perceived differently the minute you got promoted. Many of the leaders I interviewed for this book mentioned a perceived change in relational dynamics with their peers. Many young managers reported a sense of loss and loneliness when they moved into their new role. Some ceased to be invited to lunch or hang out after hours. Most young managers struggle with not being part of the 'squad' anymore and at the same time, feel out of place amongst the other managers at their level. The people with whom you used to celebrate, dream, and break the rules are the same people you will ultimately have to hold accountable.

The hardest part in transitioning into leadership is to separate from friends at work without being disconnected to them. It is also about ensuring that your peers do not get the idea that your separation is a byproduct of your new position. It's hard to tell your friends, 'We are still friends but I'm also your boss now.' As weird as this may sound, it is generally not the people who are against us that hold us back in life. It is usually the people who are the most invested in us that do. Hence, it is normal to expect key relationships turning sour when you set out on your own path. That doesn't mean that this is always the case, but many times the same people whom you were very tight with feel threatened in some way by your independence. This is where the inner conflict appears and tears you apart in opposite directions. The loss of support from peers or the loss of sponsorship from an authority figure can feel daunting.

On top of that, you are merely starting to get a handle of your new responsibilities. You will make mistakes along the way as you try to piece things together and get a hold of everything. In the process, you will experience the pain of your professional identities being stretched and tested. Usually in this process of learning, it is not difficult to feel isolated. What makes things worse is that many new managers don't ask for help because they hold on to another harmful misconception that 'Leaders must know all the answers'. No one wants to give off the idea that their promotion was a mistake. Over time, all leaders will acquire wisdom as they battle through the trials and tribulations. However, being fresh off the boat, it might be overwhelming to feel like you need to know all the answers, keep it all together, and not ask for help in case your boss perceives that to be a sign of weakness. Asking too many questions might cause the boss to lose confidence in you and think things aren't going well or that you are not in control. It is unfortunate if your leader isn't more compassionate as you are getting adjusted to your leadership role, but don't let it stop you from asking for help. All of these are concepts of the past, and while they may be only mostly imagined, it definitely helps your transition into management when you ditch these ideas right off the bat. Even then, it might be hard if your leader doesn't take kindly your naive questions.

'When you're new, you have a lot of questions, and it's important to be encouraged to ask them as much as possible. This is very tough to do when your boss isn't there or isn't an approachable person,' said Heather Taylor, twenty-nine, a social media associate at MyCorporation.com, a firm based in Calabasas, California, that helps businesses file legal documents for incorporation. 'When it's the latter quality, you often feel as though you are bothering them, especially if the questions persist after a few weeks or so.'[2]

She would wind up asking co-workers or Googling to find answers instead of talking to her manager. 'When there's no access to constant communication, you go into each day with no idea what might come next, and your behaviour changes accordingly,' Taylor said.

The key to survival is to think long term and focus on the results that are best for both parties.

This is why it is important to build your influence from the ground up. This can only be done by switching gears from focusing on personal performance to focusing on leadership. To be a well-respected leader, you will need to pick up skills that will allow you to build strong relationships with all your stakeholders, including your peers. Being lonely at the top is a consequence of not investing enough in the relationships with the different stakeholders in the workplace. The moment you spend time in building up the soft skills to nurture relationships in the long term, you will start to notice people approaching you for all sorts of issues. They begin to trust you to solve

---

[2] Overfelt, M. 21 April 2017. *What Millennials Want More Than Anything Else When They Start a New Job.* Https://Sg.Finance.Yahoo.Com/News/. Retrieved December 21, 2021, from https://sg.finance.yahoo.com/news/Millennials-want-more-anything-else-135858578.html

their problems and are eager to help you even at a short notice. The value of social capital is underrated in today's digital world and it is a noteworthy skill to invest in so that you don't end up lonely at the top. We dive deeper into this in the later chapters.

You Don't Need 'White Hair' to be Experienced

Don't confuse experience with expertise. Having faced a problem before doesn't guarantee that you've mastered the solution. Don't mistake expertise for wisdom. Having deep knowledge doesn't guarantee that you know when it applies.

—Adam Grant

There used to be an old man, in his sixties, who would go fishing even in the winter season. Every time he went, he would sit on frozen Lake Michigan, cut a hole through the ice and lower his hook to catch fish. One fine day, he was out fishing and had just completed his setup. Several hours passed, and not one single bite.

A little while later, a young man in his early twenties, listening to music, came by and sat down nearby. He cut a hole and put the hook in. The man scornfully looked at him and thought, 'I haven't caught a single fish, here comes this young punk, thinking he can out do me? Who does he think he is?'

But to his surprise, he saw the young man catch fish after fish. At first, he resisted the urge to ask the boy anything about it. His ego came in the way and he kept reminding himself that he has been fishing for over three winters now. It was too embarrassing to ask this young chap—whom he had never seen before—his secret. But the young man kept catching fish after fish, to the point he even went back to his car to get another big bucket. After resisting for a while, the old man caved in. He couldn't control himself and went to the young man and asked,

'Young man, how did you manage to catch so many fishes today? I've been sitting here for the past two hours trying to catch one and I've caught nothing. You have been here for barely twenty minutes and your buckets are so full? How?'

The young man took out his earpieces and mumbled unclearly, 'You have to keep the worms warm, Uncle,' and continued fishing. Confused, the old man asked the young man, 'What exactly do you mean by that?'

The young man looked up at the old man, pulled out the packet of worms from his mouth, and said it clearly this time,

'You have to keep the worms warm.'

The moral of the story is simple. You can have all the working experience in the world, you can work as hard as you want, but until and unless you do the right thing the right way, you won't get the desired result. Just because someone has been in an organization or industry long enough does not mean they know what they are doing and like in this story, their experience or hard work doesn't add value if they hold on to their ego and don't change with time.

When COVID-19 struck, people weren't allowed to run events like they used to. Networking events stopped, and like many others, insurance agents were forbidden to meet their prospects or clients to curb the spread of the virus. As the countries went into lockdown, many agents felt lost in their quest to bring in sales without the ability to meet people. The methods they were taught involved meeting people through roadshows, street canvassing, and referrals from existing clientele. However, with the lockdown, everything came to a standstill and many were lost in the ways to generate leads through online means. During this instance, even the most experienced personnel, the senior directors in insurance, were lost in navigating the online world to bring in new sales.

Interestingly, the ones who did better though, were the Millennials and Gen Zs who were already familiar with social media and digital marketing. They knew how to leverage the tools and technologies they had at their disposal to continue bringing in sales despite the lockdown measures.

In this case, irrelevant experience doesn't matter. The relevant experience, that gets the right kind of results, matters. There is no point in being experienced in areas that are outdated. For instance, there isn't much value in learning how to operate a pager or a fax machine in today's age. On the other hand, understanding how social media platforms like TikTok work, and leveraging those to bring in new leads, is of high value to insurance agents.

This is a common misconception everywhere, that the older you are, the more experienced you must be. In fact, the more white hairs you have, which is seen as a symbol of maturity, the more experienced you must be. However, this couldn't be further away from the truth in this day and age. With technology changing so rapidly, the older generations are finding it harder to keep up with the changes. On the other hand, the younger generation seem to be savvier with technology and keeping up with the changes is like second nature to them. Given the circumstances of the world we live in, you don't need to have white hair to have relevant experience. The younger generations today have relevant experiences in the domains that are evolving at high speed and they are better placed to guide the older generations in navigating the technological aspect of work. With COVID-19 disrupting the world and deepening our reliance on technology, we have to acknowledge that all generations have something of value to contribute to the table.

This means it is high time we ditch the notion that a younger person will not be able to provide the same amount of value to the organization compared to an older staff. Sometimes, the more you know, the less you learn. Too often experience can blind us to the new possibilities and put us on the defensive. Having a clean slate allows us to coordinate our efforts with others and accept outside input.

Challenge the Senior & Respect the Junior

This might come across as risky but trust me, it's not. Traditionally, we have been taught the opposite. Respect the senior and challenge the junior. Time to flip that on its head. In today's world, age and experience are not correlated to results achieved. You can be younger and achieve more than someone who has been in the organization five years longer than you have. Age is not the x-factor in today's age. Skill is.

I cannot tell you the number of times youths have come up to me in frustration because their bosses don't want to try out a new idea that they had which they felt would be beneficial for the organization. Back in 2019, before COVID-19 was even a thing, I was running a focus group discussion with a team in a multinational organization. This was a Millennial group that was formed to bring in new initiatives and feel heard by the management, and one of the topics they brought about was the four-day-work week. Back then, the four-day-work week was not very common and the Millennials in this focus group wanted to carry out this initiative as a trial to check if it helps to boost work–life balance and productivity. However, there was one Gen X member within the group that immediately sounded this out as a bad idea. His reasoning was, 'Yes, you can go ahead with a four-day-work week but it will be hell. You will be working much longer hours for the four days to accomplish what you normally would in five days and the experience will wear you out completely. I don't recommend trying out something we know is going to fail eventually based on simple logic.' As he was a senior within the team, no one spoke up against him and the idea was trashed immediately.

Fast forward to years later, the same organization has had to completely revolutionize the way they worked. Today, the issue their head of HR faces is in motivating their staff to come back to the office to work for all days of the week. COVID-19 has changed behaviours and people are happier with a hybrid model of work, where you meet your colleagues for a few days of the week and work from anywhere for the remaining days.

The moral of the story? Challenge the senior and respect the junior. If someone within the focus group had challenged the senior during the focus group discussion and pushed for a four-day-work week back in 2019, the transition to work from home would have been much smoother when lockdown initiatives had to come into play. Of course, no one would have known about the pandemic and the turbulence it would bring to organizations back then and yet, not pursuing progressive ways of working resulted in a loss of productivity because the organization is always behind the curve due to a lack of culture of innovation.

Similarly, many juniors are afraid to speak up early on in their career, especially if they are not confident that their leader will take their ideas positively or even be willing to acknowledge them. There have been many instances where juniors have suffered from their seniors mocking their ideas because they didn't believe in them. Not being taken seriously is an issue many juniors face. Getting people to listen to them is a common frustration reported by Millennials and Gen Z alike. Even Millennial managers struggle to get respect from both ends of the age cohort spectrum.

Here are a few verbatim remarks (positive and negative) that I've collected (from over the years of training leaders) on Millennials managing an intergenerational workforce:

- 'Generally, the younger management is less focused on micromanagement and place more emphasis on team bonding.'
- 'They feel like they know everything but honestly, they lack the experience.'
- 'They have a different perspective and approach than an older manager and may know more about recent developments, newer techniques and latest technologies.'
- 'My boss is smart but she is immature.'
- 'They are more open minded and willing to change.'
- 'They have not developed proper people skills.'
- 'They are more "with the times" and use technology to make work easier and more efficient than before.'
- 'My boss is more concerned about his own promotion and next position than mine.'

As a Millennial leader, one of the more uncommon scenarios you might find yourself in is having to manage a team of members who are older and more experienced than you are. Previously, the chances of having a team with seniors as well as juniors were pretty slim. However, because of the vast amount of change we have gone through over the years, younger leaders are now given the opportunity to lead multi-generational teams with team members who are much senior to them. In such instances, it is important that leaders challenge the norms that have been passed down from seniors and give a voice to the juniors to allow a culture of ideas and innovation to flourish.

An Iron Rice Bowl does not Motivate the Way it Used to

If you grew up in Asia, you would not be a stranger to this narrative: study hard, get into a good school, get good grades, graduate with honours and find a government job or a job with a big multinational company, and you'll be happy for the rest of your life. The iron rice bowl was portrayed as the ultimate silver bullet to all of life's problems because of the security it provided to the older generations. However, as the economy progressed and technology transformed rapidly over the years, the dreams and expectations of the Millennial generation grew with the times. A secure job alone isn't enough to keep them engaged in the workforce. The gap widened with tech companies like Google and Facebook setting a new standard for what it means to work in an organization. They provided very different incentives compared to the traditional companies and the war for talent became fierce as employees looked at jobs the same way they were shopping for products online. Millennials and Gen Zs are known to look up the employer brand of an organization to peek into the culture of the organization to see how they 'do things around here'. With websites like Glassdoor that allows existing and past employees to rate their organizations, it hasn't been difficult to get an overall objective view of how the culture of the organization is like. Organizations today need to provide more than an iron rice bowl to recruit and retain top talents in their organization.

Of course, there has been a pushback towards the Millennials and the Gen Zs for being so demanding. In fact, there have been many labels that have been placed on this generation. The most common ones include, 'entitled', 'demanding' and 'job hoppers'. Yes, it is rare to see employees stay longer than three years in any organization. The fear of the 'black mark' when you quit an organization before working there for a set number of years has faded away. We see this with the 'Great Resignation', where organizations are facing a mass exodus of talents due to multiple reasons. This was bound to happen, when management refuses to change the way they engage with their modern workforce in modern ways. Old-school strategies won't work in the new normal.

I always find it amusing when leaders mention that Millennials have no sense of loyalty to organizations like the previous generations did.

There is a big difference between being a long-term employee and a loyal employee!

Long-term employees are those who stay with the organization for a long time. They are known to work for more than five to thirty years in the same organization and are hailed as loyal employees. This is an unfair comparison because the older generation lived in harsher times where opportunities were much lesser and the consequences of quitting were much higher. Hence, the definition of a loyal employee should look only at the number of years they worked at an organization. That is a shallow way to define loyalty of an employee. Times have changed, opportunities have flourished over the years, entrepreneurship has picked up amongst many and the gig economy alone is enough to support a decent living in the world we live in today. Therefore, my definition of a loyal employee is as follows: Loyal employees are those people who are willing to turn down a better offer in a different organization to continue working with you. Loyal employees don't even bother entertaining outside opportunities from recruiters who approach them. Loyal employees are not even researching what the competition is offering compared to the market rate.

Compare the following employees:

1. Mark, fifty-nine, working in organization A for the past thirty years. He has been approached a total of three times by various recruiters since he joined organization A
2. Stacy, thirty-two, working in organization A for the past five years. She has been approached a total of ten times by various recruiters since she joined organization A.

Who is More Loyal to their Organization?

Baby Boomers and Gen Xers weren't privy to the many opportunities that Millennials and Gen Zers are exposed to today. There is a difference between staying longer in a company because you don't have better options elsewhere and being loyal to a company despite having better options elsewhere. There's little evidence to say that Baby Boomers or Gen Xers would have been as loyal had they grown up in the world

Millennials and Gen Zers did. In the old command-and-control days, fear worked really well to enforce loyalty. Fear is an effective motivator when you need people to simply comply. All you needed back then were obedient employees and everything would run smoothly. If they objected to anything, managers used fear to motivate them and the problems disappeared instantly. The problem is, because the employees back then were afraid of negative consequences such as verbal abuse or being fired, they also feared taking risks, suggesting new ideas, reporting problems and critiquing others' thinking. When people are motivated by fear, they aren't bringing their best selves to work.

Retention today is not about keeping your talents for as long as possible anymore. It is about getting them to stay longer than they usually do while making them as productive as possible the moment they join. Therefore, as Millennial leaders who understand the true meaning of loyalty, it is important to learn the psychology of motivation in order to keep the top talents in your team. This means you will have to employ a combination of intrinsic and extrinsic motivators to ensure your team members are engaged and happy within your organization. I cover more about engaging the modern workforce in the later chapters of this book.

Old school leadership tactics may not appeal to the type of workers who are more likely to help you grow in today's crowded and fiercely competitive arena. In our modern times, you may need people who can push the boundaries, people you empower to find solutions for what they need to do without waiting for the boss to tell them what to do.

Leaders who have an overly parental style may also be less likely to admit when they don't know something. Letting others see that they don't have all the answers wouldn't fit with the image of a patriarch or matriarch. Consider this: The employees of today—read Millennials and soon Gen Zs—don't necessarily expect perfection from their boss. They look for leaders who have the courage and confidence to admit that they don't have all the answers, people who are authentic and apologize when they make a mistake.

Eccentrics, mavericks, and out-of-the-box thinkers generally don't thrive in workplaces led by a leader who practices a more parental, autocratic type of leadership. These employees are likely to quickly look for the exit door once they find themselves in such environments.

One leadership style doesn't fit all. An effective leader knows to use different leadership styles for different situations. However, one form of leadership that may not survive in the workplace of the future is a style that relies on old-school leadership tactics.[3]

Employee Engagement is NOT the HR's Responsibility. It's Yours!

Every year, HR inevitably runs engagement surveys to find out how employees are feeling in that current moment. All managers want to have high employee engagement scores but in most cases, when the scores showcase a negative response, HR is usually held responsible. This is because HR have been traditionally seen as the gatekeepers of employee engagement. Since they are the ones who arrange for all matters related to people, they are held responsible even for areas that are outside their circle of control.

In essence, what we see happening is a shift of blame from leaders to HR, because it is a convenient dumping ground to do so. In reality, employee engagement shouldn't solely be the responsibility of HR—it is a shared responsibility that everyone must take up. Senior leaders need to account for the culture of the organization, and managers need to ensure their team members are immersed in their work. Employees also need to be comfortable enough with their managers and have that psychological circle of safety to be able to voice out all the issues they have in all honesty. Employee engagement isn't a one-time thing. It is silly to expect a snapshot of someone's engagement to last for the entire year. According to Gallup, managers account for over 70 per cent of the variance in employee engagement. Employees with highly engaged managers are 59% more likely to be engaged than employees supervised by actively disengaged managers.

---

[3] Martnuzzi, Bruna. 3 October 2018. 'Is It Time to Ditch These Old-School Leadership Tactics?' *American Express*. https://www.americanexpress.com/en-us/business/trends-and-insights/articles/is-it-time-to-ditch-these-old-school-leadership-tactics.

Managers play a key role in ensuring employee engagement because they have a closer relationship with employees than senior leaders and HR. Each individual is different, with unique challenges.

I remember a conversation that I had with one of my ex-classmates from my Bachelors of Psychology, Johnsen, who shared with me that he continued to stay in his toxic workplace only because his manager was fighting for the team. He had a supervisor that fought for the team, and he stayed in the organization mainly because of his leader. Being in an organization where the management doesn't understand what the others are going through on the ground was a frustrating experience, especially when his immediate superiors' hands were tied. Despite being in an environment where people were afraid of voicing their opinions because the 'truth' might not be what the big boss wants to hear, Johnsen stayed on because his immediate superior really cared for the staff, he was very on-the-ball, he took time out to listen to everyone's grievances. In fact, he was known to take time out to listen to staff even if they weren't from his department.

As a manager, you are more involved in their day-to-day work and should take responsibility in ensuring that they feel motivated. It is not the HR's responsibility to create an environment in which employees can openly discuss their work and how they are feeling. Managers need to take up ownership of dealing with people matters of their team members simply because they are the ones who are working closely with their team members. Let go of the traditional thoughts like 'Your pay cheque should be enough' to evade the responsibility of motivating your team members. Gallup has found that managers that are invested in them as people are more likely to be engaged. Take care of the people in your team. HR cannot be doing this for you.

So, What is an HR's Role?

HR plays an essential role as a facilitator to ensure all engagement initiatives are running smoothly. They support all managers and employees with the right tools and learning opportunities as well as keeping them accountable. As mentioned earlier, they are not the dumping department for all people-related issues. And they also have to ensure that the engagement initiatives that are introduced are followed through by the managers. What this implies for you, as a leader, is that you have to pick up the right competencies to deal with the different challenges you will face while working with members of your team. Sending your team members to HR is a lazy leader's move.

Chapter 3: Six Challenges in the New Normal

Emerging Trends Post Pandemic

The consequences of COVID-19 pandemic on employment, economic activity, and the way we work has been far reaching. It has affected the global labour market and the world of work which also affects the employee's well-being around the world. Based on the International Monetary Fund, global growth is estimated to have contracted by 5 per cent in 2020, representing the largest economic crisis in a generation.[4] To put this in perspective, at the onset of the pandemic, consumer spending began to decline dramatically in retail and recreation. Visits to shopping malls, restaurants, theme parks, museums, libraries, and movie theaters declined globally by almost 60 per cent. Over 15 million airline flights were cancelled and even as I write this book, a full return to pre-pandemic levels of stability seems uncertain in the short term. As a result, unemployment increased in countries affected by the COVID-19 crisis, and it has been a challenging time more particularly for workers who recently lost jobs and are in hunt of a new one amid the recession. According to the International Labour Organization (ILO), global working hours were reduced by 17.3 per cent in the second quarter of 2020. That amounts to 495 million full-time jobs lost and by the end of 2020, total working hours loss amounted to

---

[4] International Monetary Fund (2020); World Bank (2020, 2021)

roughly four times greater than the Great Recession back in 2009.[5] Global labour income declined by 8.3 per cent in 2020 which led to a 4.4 per cent global GDP, amounting to a loss of USD 3.7 trillion. Now, a new landscape of work and business is emerging from the pandemic. The days where employers seemed to hold all the cards are gone. In many industries, employees call more shots, insist on flexible working environments, and leave jobs, if necessary. In this chapter, we take a deeper look into the macro issues that you need to understand so that you can execute your role better as a leader.

1. A Dispersed Workforce

'Technology now allows people to connect anytime, anywhere, to anyone in the world, from almost any device. This is dramatically changing the way people work, facilitating 24/7 collaboration with colleagues who are dispersed across time zones, countries, and continents.'[6]

https://www.mckinsey.com/featured-insights/future-of-work/the-future-of-work-after-COVID-19

COVID-19 brought massive disruption to the workforce, highlighting the importance of physical proximity in work and spurring changes in business models and consumer behaviour, many of which are likely to endure. The physical dimension of work is a new factor shaping the future of work, brought to the fore by healthy and safety considerations. Thanks to COVID-19, dispersion will shape the new normal. Over the past decade, jobs got concentrated in the world's largest cities and people converged to them, but remote work will reverse that migration. Office vacancy rates increased significantly across major cities in 2020, by 91 per cent in San Francisco, 45 per cent in Edinburgh, 32 per cent in London, and 27 per cent in Berlin.[7]

---

[5] International labor Organization (2021)
[6] Lund, S., Madgavkar, A., Manyika, J., Smit, S., Ellingrud, K., & Robinson, O. 9 September2021. 'The future of work after COVID-19.' McKinsey & Company.
[7] Ibid.

To stop a pandemic in its tracks, countries pulled their own version of a lockdown. Companies not in essential services were ordered to ensure their employees worked from home. Millions of people scrambled to convert whatever space they could find in their homes. From rushing to get computer monitors to better chairs and even desks, the vast majority of employees have settled into a routine. They have learnt how to keep up at work while keeping in touch with colleagues. Employers and employees struggled as they navigated uncharted waters where the rules for how and where work gets done are still taking shape. Hybrid work models that let employees spend some time outside their office came with its own advantages. For instance, we can now align work experiences, locations, and individual preferences to the work itself. Both collaborative and independent tasks can be more productive, and the rigid approach will be seen as obsolete when compared to the flexible one. While most employees appreciated the flexibility and the autonomy, many also missed many aspects of being in the office, such as in-person collaboration, social interaction, and spontaneous encounters. While technology can definitely facilitate some of these moments, it cannot completely replace the in-person experience that is crucial to shaping workplace culture. This gives birth to what we now are seeing as the hybrid work model. 20 to 25 per cent of employees in advanced economies and about 10 per cent in emerging economies could work from home three to five times a week, mainly in the computer-based office work arena. This is four to five times the level before the pandemic.

A recent Gartner poll showed that 48 per cent of employees will work remotely at least part of the time after COVID-19 versus 30 per cent before the pandemic. As organizations shift to more remote work operations, there will be a complete shift in how work will get done. Most organizations are thinking of the future of work in terms of location i.e., where will we spend most of our time? Will it be in the office, at home, co-located, or distributed? There are many organizations that are advocating for the return to the traditional way of working together. But employees want something different. About 75 per cent of knowledge workers say that their expectations for working flexibly have increased. Organizations that are thinking about the future of work in a progressive way are not just evaluating where employees will be spending their time, but how they will be spending their time. We will have two options when it comes to location: co-located or distributed. We also have two modes when it comes to time spent: synchronous or asynchronous.

This gives us the four possible modes of working in the future:

	Synchronous Work	Asynchronous Work
Co-located	Working together, together. e.g., working from office with your team on a common project at the same time.	Working alone, together. e.g., working from office but on your own work project that doesn't require your team's involvement at different times.
Distributed	Working together, apart. e.g., working from home on a common project while being connected via online meeting platforms at the same time.	Working alone, apart. e.g., working from home on your own work project that doesn't require your team's involvement at different times.

According to Gartner, HR leaders rank synchronous work modes as more important to team innovation. This is because we are still operating in a culture of meetings. However, Gartner posits that asynchronous work is as important as synchronous work. Individuals need deep-focused time to restore their mental energy. Organizations need to invest more in the asynchronous modes that contribute equally to innovation. Sadly, only 17 per cent of organizations have implemented no-meeting days and only 11 per cent of organizations have provided dedicated mental health days, and only 1 per cent have implemented no-email days. Organizations that want to succeed in future must invest equally in all four modes of work and empower teams to collaborate across each.

This means they will have to reconfigure their onsite spaces so that when we are working together in the same physical location, we have the right environments to carry out collaboration efforts in person. They will also mean they have to understand how third-party locations can come into play; such as cafes or co-working offices that can encourage employees to network with one another for those moments where we are working in-person in the same physical space, albeit on different projects. Companies will also need to equip employees with the tools and technologies to make the virtual experience of working together from home less straining and more intentional. Really progressive organizations and leaders will also empower their employees to make full use of their time, working alone on their own personal projects in any location such as their homes or any other location for that matter. Whether employees decide to go to the gym, meditate, or spend time as they feel fit, it is accepted as a mode of working that allows the employees to rejuvenate themselves and re-fuel their tank on a regular basis. As the world continues to work in a dispersed realm, hybrid working is the way forward. Hybrid working expands the number of modes of working that are crucial to innovation. organizations that improve the access to all of these modes and invest in improving the quality of each mode will truly drive performance in the hybrid environment. The pandemic will eventually fade, but the agility and creativity of policymakers and businesses evident during the pandemic will need to continue, to find effective responses to the looming workplace challenges.

Hub-and-spoke Model

This is not a new concept, but it is becoming more popular now with the hybrid working model being the norm. The hub-and-spoke model simply means there will be a headquarter serving as the hub of the business, and there will be spokes that are a geographically distributed network of offices, created on the basis of talent and client needs.

The hub is usually found in a central location with excellent access to public transport. Office spaces will now primarily become a space that caters for collaboration as virtual events are not as effective for activities such as brainstorming. The arrangement of spoke offices across different locations gives employees the flexibility to work not only closer to home but to also cut commute times which generally boost work–life balance, and often results in a happier workforce. This model is also good to ignite local economies, creating local jobs and expanding the talent pool which might have then otherwise been restricted to more central locations. Companies have the opportunity to reimagine how and where work is done, thinking through specific work arenas and occupational activities. Speedy and effective worker redeployment will be needed by recruiting and retaining workers based on skills and experience over academic degrees. Search for Common Ground, a nonprofit organization, with more than 500 employees globally, has operated under the hub-and-spoke model since 2018. This approach enabled the organization to reduce its office space by 65 per cent and optimize the employee experience through the modernization of its communication tools, design, and technology. Flexibility has become the No. 1 requirement for key talent when considering joining a company, and demand for flexibility will doubtless continue. By establishing new spokes—satellite offices in other cities—a company gains greater access to talent located beyond its hub city. Companies that foster flexible work arrangements will benefit by attracting top-shelf candidates—as well as increased productivity, profitability, and loyalty from their current workforce. The impact of the hub-and-spoke model is also significant in terms of a company's environmental impact—a growing concern of many employees. Downsizing to a smaller hub can shrink a company's carbon footprint by lowering the amount of energy expended on appliances, air-conditioning and heating, as well as emissions from commuting employees' vehicles.

Challenges You Will Face as a Leader

Much of the new workplace is undoubtedly hybrid. Organizations that refuse to allow at least some remote work will have to watch talent walk out of the door. During this period, you will have to learn how to balance and make the best of both worlds. What this means for you as the leader of a team is to have an experimental mindset with the hybrid modes. Hybrid work modes need constant support and refinement for it to work effectively and you have to be willing to try different permutations and combinations to figure out the sweet spot where work gets done well and on time, without burning out your team. Middle managers have borne the brunt of work during the pandemic and will continue to do so in a hybrid and remote work setting. You will have to attend virtual meetings to hear top management's decisions and then communicate the same to your team members. After that, you will have the task of ensuring ground operations run smoothly in compliance with the ever-changing regulations. In such situations, you have to be prepared to motivate your team members when you yourself are feeling overwhelmed.

Think about it

- Which of the four modes have I worked in already and which ones do I need to experiment with?
- Which of the four modes do I get the most work done in?
- Which of the four modes do I enjoy working the most in?
- How can I leverage and collaborate within the four modes of working to get the most out of my team members?
- How will you conduct an appraisal for employees who work in a hybrid workplace?

A Burnt-out Workforce

'Burnout is not an individual problem. It is an organizational problem. We can fight it with demand-control-support:

1) Reduce the demands of the job
2) Give people more control over them
3) Make sure they have support to cope with them' [8]

---

[8] Adam Grant, Author of *Think Again*.

If you were feeling a little overwhelmed with work during the pandemic, fret not, you were not alone. People everywhere carved out socially distant routines that, for many, blurred the line between personal and professional lives. Similarly, employers accepted the forced experiment to be flexible and trusted that business could still function as usual. Amidst all the turbulence, organizations had the chance to co-create better cultures with their employees. Those who chose to seize it took steps to elevate the employee experience. The progressive companies were quick to notice it and implement it on the ground. Nike, LinkedIn, and Bumble started it off by giving their workers a paid week-off. Citigroup banned work calls on Fridays. Scotland is working its way towards a four-day workweek without a loss of pay. As organizations adopted a remote work arrangement, they started to see the effects of working from home through their employees. Regrettably, many other organizations didn't take the same steps. And to a certain extent, most companies are still struggling to face the conundrums that force them to question their current methods of working. The truth is, as much as it is tempting to yearn for pre-pandemic modes of thinking and working, these organizations have less to offer the candidates and their existing employees.

Why Were Employees Burning out When They Could Work from Home?

When you think of working from home, it is easy to imagine a cozy picture, almost like the laptop entrepreneur sipping his pina colada while sitting at the beach in Hawaii. Contrary to traditional thinking, where working from home equals to slacking or doing the bare minimum, working from home was actually pretty draining for many employees despite the conveniences that came with it. Yes, it meant more time with family members. Yes, it meant they could take some time out to run some errands. But it also meant that people had to work after working hours with expectations for them to respond to emails way past working hours. As countries issued lockdown orders and companies shifted to remote work, individuals went through chaos. The struggle from figuring out how to productively work from home to worrying about being made redundant to working longer hours from home has made an impact on the employees. Because adults spend the bulk of their time working, the workplace is naturally one environment facing fresh challenges in a new normal. The sheer length of the pandemic, combined with the yo-yo effect of good news followed by bad news, are stressors that have burnt employees out. Even unmarried, fully remote workers went through feelings of isolation and loneliness. Whether you found yourself spending more time with your devices, or screaming at your kids at home, or missing the company of your friends and family, there were plenty of unique pandemic-related problems to go around. It has been a mad rollercoaster for many.

Burnout isn't Just About Feeling Exhausted

While it may seem similar, burnout is not purely about feeling exhausted. We might think that burnout is the result of sitting at our desk for too long, attending too many virtual meetings, and never catching a break. But that's not all there is to burnout, that's just exhaustion! Exhaustion is just the first stage. Researchers say that exhausted employees still believe in themselves and the work that they do. They are simply too tired to attend to it. Many of my friends have commented that they now work longer hours and feel the need to respond to emails late into the night. Moreover, a 24/7 organizational culture drains employees and gives them little opportunity to recharge. With such an overload evolving into a chronic job condition, it is no surprise that employees find themselves too depleted to even clear simple tasks. This is when they become cynical about themselves, their company and the workload they have. The prolonged sense of exhaustion leads employees to feel incompetent and stuck in their jobs. This hurts their morale and leads to the fear of not contributing meaningfully, and adds on to their feelings of inadequacy.

The notion that the holidays should be the time to recharge is flawed! The holidays should be a time to celebrate. If work is exhausting people to the point that they are using their time off to recover, exhaustion is bound to transform into burnout in such working cultures. A healthy organization doesn't leave people drained in the first place. Those struggling with inefficacy have enough energy and care about their job, but don't feel validated by their contributions. This state of persistent fatigue arises when employees are buried with too much work to complete with limited resources and little control over their environment. This is the tipping point that turns exhaustion into burnout.

Feeling Blah?

Adam Grant, organizational psychologist and renowned author, put a name to the feeling we experienced that didn't fit the full description of burnout. He called it languishing, after he found out more about it from friends who struggled with concentrating on projects. It wasn't burnout as many felt energy and it wasn't depression either because many still held on to the feeling of hope. This middle-ground feeling was a mix of being joyless and aimless, a sense of stagnation and emptiness, and it is known as languishing. This term was coined by sociologist Corey Keys who used it to describe people who weren't depressed and at the same time weren't thriving. The challenge with this feeling is that it can happen unnoticed by many. It is difficult to catch yourself slipping slowly into solitude or even notice the dulling of delight or the dwindling of your drive. As the pandemic continues to drag on, the state of anguish is morphing into a chronic condition of languish. In the past few years, even before the pandemic, people were habitually checking email seventy-four times a day and switching tasks every ten minutes. However, due to the pandemic, many employees have also had to deal with interruptions from kids around the house, colleagues around the world and bosses around the clock. Therefore, 'not depressed' does not mean you are not languishing. 'Not burned out' does not mean you're fired up either. There is an in-between space that leaders need to be aware of, and be able to detect within themselves and their team members in order to lead them through the years ahead.[9]

---

[9] Grant, A. 3 December2021, 'Feeling Blah During the Pandemic? It's Called Languishing'. *The New York Times*. https://www.nytimes.com/2021/04/19/well/mind/COVID-mental-health-languishing.html

Bad Leadership Makes Burnout Worse

Things head for a downturn when employees are not supported properly by their leader and the organization. An overall work culture that promotes presenteeism will discourage employees from taking leave or utilizing the wellness initiatives that have been rolled out by the organization. This defeats the purpose of creating such wellness initiatives in the first place. If stressors like discrimination, bias or unfairness exist within the organization, employees are bound to withdraw. The sad reality for many organizations is employees shy away from speaking to their bosses about their personal struggles for fear of being seen as weak or even worse, stigmatized. Research shows that 60% with a mental illness do not seek treatment because they worry about the impact it might have in hurting their careers.

Stop Sweeping Mental Health Issues under the Carpet

This is made even worse if the leaders have an outdated mentality about speaking up about 'personal issues at work'. This is one of the fixed mindsets that needs to shift to really showcase true leadership. If leaders are only concerned about the work produced by their employee, and are not interested in listening to their 'personal issues' that may affect their quality of work, then are we really treating our employees humanely? Such treatment may work for machines, but sweeping issues around mental health under the carpet will not make the issues around burnout go away. We cannot expect employees and colleagues to thrive professionally when they are struggling personally. A holistic approach to wellbeing demands that leaders be attentive to the needs of the whole person. This is an iceberg problem, where the main issue is hidden below the surface. The circumstances of working from home doesn't allow the leader to be able to read the non-verbal signs as clearly as they could in person. When bosses cannot meet their colleagues in person as often as they would like to, they cannot have conversations to detect the red flags that may point to burnout within their team members. It is much harder for leaders to get a sense of how their colleagues are coping when everyone is working remotely. All of these issues are bringing into sharper focus a greater burden for the leader to pick up the pieces and level up in the way they engage with their team members.

The Well-being–Engagement Paradox

Research by Gallup's wellbeing-engagement paradox of 2020 has shown that engagement and well-being are linked and known to be reciprocal. In other words, the higher the employee engagement, the better the well-being of the employee. It used to function in a directly proportional manner in the pre-pandemic days. When employees are engaged and thriving at work, burnout decreases and productivity increases.

However, in 2020, employee engagement and well-being diverged and went separate ways. This divergence presents critical implications for the workplace leaders in the coming years. Many expected employee engagement to plunge as a result of hardships caused by the pandemic. Yet, in contrast to well-being, employee engagement actually increased overall in 2020. Despite experiencing new kinds of stress and worry each day, many employees have been steadfast through COVID-19 and showcased their efforts, enthusiasm, and commitment during this period. During the layoffs and furloughs, employees were grateful to still have a job, experience the benefits of increased flexibility and autonomy by working from home, and appreciated the leadership efforts from management that put in efforts to rally the employees and engage them to stay afloat. Employees during this initial phase were inspired by and united by a shared sense of purpose.[10]

Since engagement levels were notably high, it is easy to expect wellness scores to be high as well, as that was the way engagement influenced wellness during the pre-pandemic days. Unfortunately, that has not been the case because remote working intensified engagement as well as the negative emotions such as stress, worry, and fear. Many employees were forced home with little to no warning while actively working to reduce sources of exceptional stress and worry. Many went

---

[10] Wigert Ben, Sangeeta Agrawal, Kristin Barry, and Ellyn Maese. 13 March 2021. 'The Wellbeing–Engagement Paradox of 2020'. *Gallup.* https://www.gallup.com/workplace/336941/wellbeing-engagement-paradox-2020.aspx.

through social isolation and restriction due to the restrictions imposed by the government authorities. The fact that many employees had no idea how to structure their remote work effectively and had little guidance on that matter only worsened their feelings of stress and panic. Moreover, there is a big difference between being trapped at home in contrast to having the flexibility to choose to work from home.

Hence, the extremely polarizing work-life experiences resulting from the pandemic has left many employees hitting or approaching a breaking point that leads to burnout and suffering with long-term consequences. Negative emotions like stress and worry spiked in the early months of the pandemic and sustained high levels that continued to drain the fortitude of the employees. This is an important insight for leaders: when managing remote teams during the pandemic, leaders need to capitalize on the advantages of working from home, while actively working to reduce sources of exceptional stress and worry. This is why it is important for leaders to engage employees and fend off chronically high levels of stress and worry. Leaders who work proactively to prevent and manage burnout while capitalizing on the needed flexibility and efficiency that comes with remote work will be able to develop stronger, healthier, and more productive workforces in the future. We have to keep in mind that even as the economy recovers, it will not be a sustainable recovery unless the leaders ensure a holistic approach towards well-being recovery amongst their people.[11] Strategies to deal with burnout and other similar issues will be covered in chapter 8.

Challenges You Will Face as a Leader

Whether your employees are returning to the office, or staying remote for the long-term, or have worked in the office throughout the pandemic, their experiences, in general, have changed. Which of those experiences should stay, and which should continue to evolve?

---

[11] Beheshti, Naz. 15 April 2021. 'The Pandemic Has Created a New Kind of Burnout, Which Makes Well-being More Critical Than Ever'. *Forbes*. https://www.forbes.com/ sites/nazbeheshti/2021/04/15/the-pandemic-has-created-a-new-kind-of-burnout-which-makes-well-being-more-critical-than-ever/?sh=75abb82b2f01.

How can you, as a leader, create peak and other positive experiences that meet your team's needs whether they're physically in the office or elsewhere? More importantly, how will you be able to ensure your team retains its productivity levels or even exceeds it without compromising on well-being? What can you do to help a team member struggling with mental health issues to get through a difficult time?

Think about it

- Do you currently have a psychological circle of safety in your team where people can open up to you as a leader?
- How comfortable are your team members in opening up to you and admitting the fact that their mental health is taking a toll? Ask them to rate you on a scale of 1–10 and probe further based on their answers to get clear answers.
- How will you identify if your team members are exhausted, languishing, or burnt out when they are working remotely?
- How can you ensure you are not contributing to burnout? What can you start, stop, or continue to do?
- How are you helping your team relax, recuperate, and rejuvenate?
- How will you keep the morale up for your team when individuals start leaving?

The Great Resignation

'The Great Resignation isn't a mad dash away from the office. It's the culmination of a long march toward freedom.

Flexibility is more than choosing the place where you work. It's having freedom to decide your purpose, your people, and your priorities.'

—Adam Grant

At the onset of the pandemic, many employees were worried about losing their jobs and perhaps because of that, many started proactively looking for a back-up plan. A survey conducted by the Achievers Workforce Institute in the US and Canada indicated that more than half intended to look for a new job. In Singapore, a *Michael Page Talent Trends* report similarly found that 56 per cent of employed respondents are expecting to find a new job. This is despite the Singapore economy seeing a contraction of 2 per cent in the second quarter of 2020. This shows the level of pent-up frustration employees were facing in their current working environment to consider leaving even when opportunities to get another job were so low.

Unfortunately, the statistics and trends are indicating that leaders do not have an accurate pulse of the sentiments of employees on the ground. The obvious telltale sign is through what has unfolded as the 'Great Resignation'. As community cases started tapering down in the respective countries, companies started calling their employees back to the office once the restrictions were lifted. When Singapore issued its first phase of lockdown, the wife of my friend related how almost every department in their organization decided to go remote except hers. That too, when her department wasn't even rendering an essential service, which meant work from home was the legal thing to do. However, because the department head didn't like the idea of working from home, he ended up ordering the team to the office. When complaints to the human resource department did nothing of consequence, a few anonymous calls to the Ministry of Manpower helped change things. When leaders take the law in their own hands, one can't help but wonder what is going on in their heads!

According to McGregor's theory of managing people, in theory X, the average person is assumed to dislike work and avoid all responsibilities when possible. Leaders who subscribe to this school of thought believe that the threat of punishment is needed for workers to do their work as assigned. This type of management probably might apply to an assembly line of factory workers, but definitely is a struggle when you are trying to manage people working remotely. Leaders who were managed like this by their own bosses may find it challenging to give up the urge to manage their staff in the same manner, and hence, demand them to be in the office in a physical setting. Of course, these kinds of poor leadership practices are not new. The pandemic simply put the spotlight on the fault lines and highlighted the key issues that needed dire attention. Leaders who don't respect boundaries are the very same people who send after-work emails and messages and act as if it is the norm, and expect their team members to operate at the same tempo. In Singapore, the average employee is known to be putting in forty-four hours per week and Singapore is infamous for being at the bottom ten for work–life balance by a study from tech company Kisi and ranked the second most overworked in a study of forty cities.[12]

As work from home continues to be the primary mode of work, these types of managers are looking for workarounds to implement their ancient approach of measuring performance. Examples of such behaviour include scheduling video calls around lunchtime so that employees cannot go for long lunches or expecting employees to 'take attendance' by submitting their 'good morning' messages via WhatsApp every day or even setting the expectation for all team members to have the webcam turned on for the entire day, based on the pretext that it brings people together and makes them feel more connected.

Leaders, Stop Pretending the Internet Doesn't Exist

Companies have for far too long ignored the powerful technologies that have unleashed this ability for us to work from home. Many people managers are not trained and equipped with the skills to measure outcomes and performance of the people working in a virtual setting. Hence, they regress to measuring time spent by checking in their clock-in and clock-out times as well as measuring how long they were out for lunch or if the employee left earlier than the boss. When everyone was forced to work from home, people managers started freaking out because commanding and controlling their people became impossible. 'Are you working?', 'Are you watching Netflix?', 'Are you taking a nap?'—these are the questions that went through their head and stressed them out. Going back to the office allowed them to keep tabs on people based on time spent as opposed to work done.

What this illustrates to many is that our leaders are not fully equipped to level up and manage a remote team effectively. They have

[12] Tan, A. 31 May 2021. 'Commentary: Why do some bosses still want their workers to come back to the office?' *CNA*. https://www.channelnewsasia.com/commentary/work-from-home-bosses-COVID-19-breaches-office-2082756

been so entrenched in managing in archaic ways of the past that they are now struggling to mend their ways of management. This means, they are unable to be agile, to unlearn and relearn in order to work in a volatile, uncertain, complex and ambiguous (VUCA) world. When a knowledge-working team has to work from home, suddenly the manager's skills, their ability to manage work, and the creative output from the team is put into sharper focus. If this manager isn't used to organizing work, to balancing workflows, aligning individual work with each other, the by-product that we see is that the team's productivity suffers. When a leader doesn't have the skills to put in place the management mechanisms, to make the team run smoothly as possible as a team, the problem of a lack of productivity lies with the leader. This might be very difficult for the leader to accept, so they revert back to their old ways of management—come back to work from the office or simply put the blame back on their team members by accusing them of not working productively from home. Leaders need to be the ones who take up the responsibility of motivating their team members, find newer ways to align the work they are doing with the schedules they are up against. Leaders need to be skilled in managing people based on performance from a distance.

The role models of leaders that employees enjoy working under have mentioned that their leaders are more concerned that they may be overworking themselves while working from home because there's no official signal to tell them to stop work for the day. In fact, these leaders are known to schedule short one-on-one check-in sessions either before lunch or before work 'officially ends' to tell them to go for their lunch or to tell them to take a break for the rest of the day and not continue working because work is perpetual—there will always be work that needs to get done. Otherwise, it is possible to have employees working twelve to thirteen hours a day.

Thus, when certain companies are calling their employees to go back to a five-day work week completely from the office, that was a trigger for many to throw in their resignation letters. Many loathe the bane of rush-hour commute, the loss of the newfound autonomy, and the painful practicalities of having to wear a mask while at office.

Employees have invested in home offices, better internet connections, webcams, microphones, and so much more to make working from home an ease. It has also given employees more time to spend with their family. So they're not really as willing to give it all back. When things hit a tipping point, people do the very thing that they have been contemplating ever since the first lockdown: 'Should I just quit?'

Remote Work Has Opened Doors of Opportunities

Before the pandemic, according to a 2017 survey by the Society of Human Resource Management, the top factors that typically drove employees to switch jobs were compensation and benefits, job security, and growth opportunities. Job satisfaction was already at a low of 59 per cent. While the top factors haven't changed much, employees are expecting more from their leaders. The global economy is larger than ever, but just having a job is no longer the most important thing. The lockdown in 2020 triggered a common pattern of soul-searching amongst many employees. According to Tabitha, a Millennial who had spent the last few years in IT engineering, it was the perfect opportunity to jump: 'The job I was doing was soul-crushing work. The pandemic woke me up to that. I started questioning why I was doing this to myself. Now, I feel more hopeful and I feel like I'm finally working towards the goals I had set with my life.'

Management professor Anthony Klotz at Texas A&M University, who coined the phrase 'The Great Resignation', says, 'When we come in contact with life-threatening events, we tend to reflect on death and consider whether we are happy with our lives or we would like to make changes to them. The pandemic forced people to take stock of their lives and gave them the opportunity to reimagine it.'[13]

Several surveys are showing that many people are still thinking about quitting. Some may be looking for a career break due to burnout

---

[13] Miller, A. 8 January 2022, 'A&M professor who predicted 'Great Resignation' explains potential factors of why theory came true.' *The Eagle*. https://theeagle.com/news/a_m/a-m-professor-who-predicted-great-resignation-explains-potential-factors-of-why-theory-came-true/article_e99bb37c-6f29-11ec-9a2e-030d1c45b621.html

brought on by the pandemic, others may be searching for more purpose and meaning in their jobs, and some may simply want to continue working remotely at least part of the time or simply a higher paycheck.

Research from Engagerocket shows that out of 2600 respondents, 72 per cent of workers in Singapore would prefer to continue to work from home at least 50 per cent of the time, given the flexibility and higher productivity levels they experienced.[14]

Most employees have become used to working from home and have created their unique work spaces that allow them to be more productive. As the pandemic worsened, flexible work schedules and supportive management became even more important. With the ever-changing workplace restrictions, employees have come to value time and location more than ever before. Even the role of the leaders has increased, in terms of importance, to an even higher degree. According to researchers Wigert & Barrett, the more employees work from home, the more likely they are to depend on their leaders' frequent contact. From the onset of the crisis, many employees have reported feeling unprepared to fulfill their responsibilities which underscores the need for good communication between leaders and their team members.

The massive dip in employment rates after the first lockdowns of 2020 is now bigger than ever and it is predicted to rise.[15]

The Great Resignation is a growing movement that is urging people to quit their jobs en masse. According to a study by Monster, over 95 per cent of employees in the United States are thinking about changing their jobs. Additionally, this number does not include the 4 million people who have already quit their jobs so far. Meanwhile, another survey from asset management company Mercer, showed that while there was a significant increase in employee turnover in the first half of 2021 compared to the same period in 2020, there was also 'a resurgence

---

[14] Tan, A. 31 May 2021. 'Commentary: Why do some bosses still want their workers to come back to the office?' *CNA*. https://www.channelnewsasia.com/commentary/work-from-home-bosses-COVID-19-breaches-office-2082756

[15] 9 November 2021. 'Breezy Explainer: What is the Great Resignation 2021? Why Millions of Employees Are Quitting?'. *Zee5*. https://www.zee5.com/articles/breezy-explainer-what-is-the-great-resignation-2021-why-millions-of-employees-are-quitting

in hiring for Singapore companies due to a rise in replacement hiring (51 per cent), business expansion (30 per cent) and the opening of roles which were previously on hiring freeze (15 per cent).' This is bad news for firms that are struggling to stay afloat.

There are several reasons behind employees wanting to quit but the main reason is that employees are unwilling to continue working in an organization that requires them to go back and work in the office for all working days of the week. Several people have transitioned into working remotely and are enjoying the quality of life that it offers. On the other hand, several people used the downtime from the pandemic to upskill and are now looking to incorporate their interests into their work. Others are interested in roles that give them more time, while some just don't want work that eats away at their pleasure. The balance of power has shifted from the employers to the employees.

Employees want the best of both worlds. Around 73 per cent prefer the option of working remotely whereas 67 per cent want more physical interactions with their colleagues.[16]

People no longer want to settle and are being very picky when it comes to their job search. Most of those who are quitting have enough in their savings to tide them over a period of unemployment with a backup plan after they quit.

The hybrid model provides much of the balance and flexibility that employees enjoyed for over a year, as well as the social interaction that they missed. It is being seen as a viable alternative that still meets the requirements of safety, efficiency, versatility, and connection. The hybrid workplace model cannot be a one-size-fits-all approach, and it requires adaptability from both the employee and the employer.

The result of the Great Resignation has been obvious. Employers have been scrambling to retain and attract employees. They are offering retention bonuses, allowing employees to work remotely forever, and offering new benefits to support employees' personal and professional development. Some are even instituting policies to help workers recover

---

[16] O.C. Tanner Institute. (2022). *Rethink 2022 Global Culture Report*. O.C. Tanner. https://www.octanner.com/content/dam/oc-tanner/images/v2/culture-report/2022/home/INT-GCR2022.pdf.

from burnout, whether it is a sabbatical, closing the company for a week, or shrinking the workweek from five days to four.[17]

Evidently, the huge wave of resignations spurred by the pandemic has forced companies to confront burnout, implementing 'burnout breaks' to curb the loss of productivity that comes with working too much.

Challenges You Will Face as a Leader

As a leader, it is not only about ensuring employees have the technology-related tools to work efficiently from home but the human touch in supporting the staff during this tumultuous period. Are you listening well to your employees and giving regular feedback? Are you putting in effort to get to know your employees better and being creative with the employee experiences you can design for them? Also, are you recognizing the efforts put in by your employees beyond compensation and benefits? Sometimes all it takes is a simple and sincere visible gesture to show that they make a positive difference to you and the company. The key is to keep all of these in mind as employees have realized that there are better alternatives out there. If they do not wish to work in a toxic or unpleasant working environment, they can choose not to. Technology has empowered the gig economy which has in turn allowed for employees to source for part-time roles to sustain themselves. Retaining your talent pool will require you to be creative and on your toes as a leader. Being a lazy leader may have worked very well in the past, but it is a surefire formula for disaster in the new normal.

Think about it

Most leaders confuse what it means to listen. Listening is not about hearing the words that were said. It is about **making someone feel heard. Do your team members feel heard when they speak with**

---

[17] Fox, M. 4 November 2021. November. 'The 'Great Resignation' is altering the workforce dynamic—maybe for good.' *CNBC*. https://www.cnbc.com/2021/11/01/great-resignation-may-be-altering-workforce-dynamic-for-good.html

you? How employers address mental well-being issues reveal the relationship between the leaders and the employees, and underscores a deeper picture of the overall company culture. As a leader, you will be observed by the way you handle retrenchment.

- Are you listening to your employees keenly, making them feel heard, and taking follow-up action based on their feedback?
- Are you listening to respond, or listening to understand when you do listen to your employees?
- Are your employees suffering from longer work hours in front of the computer, heavier workloads, endless zoom meetings, and a myriad of other new responsibilities that are wearing them out?
- When employees decide to leave, are you seen as treating them with respect and dignity?
- When employees are suffering from loneliness in isolation, do you do anything to help?
- Have you tried any new interventions to ensure your employees' mental health is protected under your care?
- How are you allowing flexibility in a hybrid model while meeting the unique needs and expectations of your hybrid team members?
- How can you keep your team members engaged?
- How are you going to ensure they feel listened to and valued, and appreciated?
- How and where can your team members work, and how can you best support them?

The Gig Economy and the Rise of the Micropreneur

'Now we have a gig economy where many people are holding down several jobs at once. The whole concept of 40-hour workweek makes people under 30 laugh.'
        —Katrina Onstad, Author of 'The Weekend Effect

Long before lockdown, the OECD Future of Work study had predicted that 50 per cent of developed country workforces would be gig workers by 2030. Many white-collar professionals thought that was not referring to them but rather to the Uber and Grab drivers, the virtual assistants, or the freelance instructors and the like. With COVID-19, e-commerce and other virtual transactions started booming. This created an increased demand for gig work. Many consumers experienced the convenience of e-commerce, grocery delivery ordered by an app, and other online activities during the pandemic. In 2020, the share of e-commerce in retail sales grew at two times the rate before COVID-19, increasing its share of total retail sales by several multiples. More than three-quarters of people using digital channels for the first time during the pandemic say that they will continue using them even in the new normal. This shift to digital transactions has propelled growth in delivery, transportation, and warehouse jobs, while setting off declines among in-store jobs such as cashiers. Retail brick-and-mortar shops are closing while Amazon hired 400,000 workers worldwide during the pandemic. In China, e-commerce, delivery, and social media jobs rose by more than 5.1 million during the first half of 2020. Many of the jobs created in long-haul transportation and last-mile delivery comes via the gig economy. The growth of e-commerce and other digital transactions are indicating a shift to gig jobs in the independent workforce.

The independent workforce provides the flexibility and freedom that many workers with other commitments require and during the pandemic, it was a safety net for individuals who resigned or were retrenched. In India, the gig economy grew rapidly in 2020 across all platforms. In China, many waiters, cooks, administrative staff, and many other workers who lost jobs during COVID-19 found new work in the gig economy. In this era of chronic skill shortages, rapid automation, digital transformation and the impending 'Great Resignation', companies are confronting a growing talent problem that has the potential to become a strategic bottleneck. Finding the right people with the right skills to do the right work at just the right time will be a new challenge that leaders will have to face. The half-life of skills is shrinking fast, and many jobs now come and go in a matter of years.

New platforms like Catalent, Innocentive, Kaggle, Toptal, and Upwork are emerging and offering on-demand access to highly skilled workers. This includes anybody from big-data scientists to strategic project managers, and even interim CEOs and CFOs. These experts may be hired for strategic initiatives or embedded in teams, and the projects they are assigned to can range in length from a few hours to a few years. The COVID-19 crisis is increasingly turning companies towards this kind of platform.

Today, almost all Fortune 500 companies use one or more of them. These platforms provide workers who have four-year college degrees or advanced degrees that represent an understudied element of the emerging gig economy. It is not much of a surprise to see companies leveraging high-skills platforms in large numbers as the pandemic has shown us how they can increase labor force flexibility, accelerate time to market, and enable innovation. They are seeking help with projects that are short and long term, tactical and strategic, specialized and general. It is believed by the C-suite leaders that these platforms will be central to their ability to compete in the new normal.

Millions of well-qualified professionals today are attracted to contract work. Freelancers are now estimated to make up a third of the US workforce and for the first time since 2014, freelancers who say they consider gig work to be a long-term career choice are the same number that consider it a temporary way to make money. Early signs suggest that the pandemic will speed up this shift. Much of the shift is the result of the demographic changes that have been underway for four or five decades but little has been done till now by traditional organizations to address the issues.

As we see more Millennial employees entering the 'sandwich-generation' phase, where they have to take care of their parents and their offsprings, they value the flexibility of time to be able to work from home and work around the errands they need to run. Life gets in the way and it is difficult to manage both without hiring outside help if flexibility is not a key part of the equation. When burdened with childcare or eldercare, many employees are dropping out of the workforce to manage their responsibilities back home. The gig economy allows them to reduce the financial impact of not having a full-time job by allowing them to work in the time they can allocate within their busy schedules. The gig economy allows them the flexibility to handle their family obligations while delivering quality work.

Even highly skilled and experienced women who take time off to have children and for other life events are finding it difficult to restart their careers or are seeing themselves get sidetracked in traditional organizations. Statistics from a 2009 Center for Work-Life Policy Survey shows that more than two-thirds of 'highly qualified' women with advanced degrees or MBAs drop out of the workforce because they don't have access to more flexible job arrangements. Online talent platforms allow them to more smoothly transition into the workforce once they have taken their time out to care for their familial obligations.

The gig economy is also a boon to the Boomers—especially workers who are laid off or edged out of traditional firms once they hit a certain age. These platforms allow for these experienced talents to offer them a way to continue to use their skills and experience while maintaining work–life balance. Given that we are going to be experiencing an aging population in many countries, gig platforms like UpWork expect to see more experienced workers with hard-to-find-skills delay retirement by working on a part-time basis. This is not only useful for them financially, but it also provides them with an activity to keep themselves busy and occupied in their golden years without much stress.

Decomposition of Job Roles

Historically, companies hired permanent white-collar employees for a number of reasons. Firstly, it was hard to find good talent, so when you did find them, it made sense to lock them in. Most companies operated in their own unique ways so it took a lot of time to induce new employees to do things their way in their organizational culture. Lastly, in a world where monitoring quality was hard, it was important for employers to trust their employees to not steal from the company or neglect quality. This could only be ensured if they were long-term employees. Similarly, for employees, they join permanent roles because that is the only way to progress. In order to be promoted, you needed to stay a while with the organization. And back in those days, there used to be a pension scheme that paid employees for their retirement. The longer you stayed in an organization, the better the pension benefits were. Back then, changing employers was considered unethical, and it could leave a black mark on you. Employers till today are known to threaten employees by smearing their name across the board so that none of their competitors would hire them. This made employees less employable elsewhere. Last but not least, employees too had a fixed mindset back then. In the pre-internet world, a huge amount of information wasn't codified. It was learnt on the job and was considered company or industry specific. Hence, it was hard to learn transferable skills that could allow you to move across companies, industries, or functions.[18]

Slowly, things have changed over the decades. From 'jobs for life' to 'jobs for a few years' to 'jobs for a few weeks'. As the gig economy grows, one thing that we can expect to see from companies is the decomposition of job roles. When a company decides to turn core functions over to freelance workers, the job roles are broken down into smaller competencies. Most companies haven't focused on this yet as in traditional workplaces, leaders can afford to be vague when delegating work assignments. Leaders know that everyone on the project team will be interacting so frequently that they will be able to clarify goals and make course corrections over time. However, when working with talents from the gig platforms, they have to provide much of the information upfront. Therefore, leaders need to be open minded to buy into this concept of delegating work to freelancers when it becomes hard to find talent.

Companies will need to get leaders to see how they personally can benefit from talent platforms. There are a lot of things in your day-to-day work that you can offload so that you can do higher order work. As more teams include full time and gig employees, working norms will change with it. Leaders will have to deal with seeing a different skilled individual turning up to the office or on zoom to complete the project if the freelancer is unavailable for that particular day. They will need to step into coach and connector roles and learn how to work productively

---

[18] Legg, Ben. ' Portfolio careers Are Becoming the New Normal'. *Digital People International.* https://www.digitalpeople.online/portfolio-career

across dispersed, often remote teams. Collaboration would be a key skill that leaders will need while dealing with a revolving set of teammates articulating previously tacit team norms and making progress simple for all to track.

Career Portfolios Beats Career Paths

We are used to thinking about work in terms of jobs. But with the nature and structure of work changing rapidly, this may no longer be helpful. Successful organizations are shifting their thinking towards the capabilities needed to win in their marketplace. Through strategic modeling of future workforce options, they clarify the future roles, skills, and mindsets to deliver their strategy. They then focus on sourcing and developing these through reskilling, upskilling, recruitment or drawing on the wider 'gig economy' of flexible workers.

In an environment of ongoing uncertainty, employers will be even more attracted to the gig economy route for a variety of reasons: it makes hiring easier for hard-to-fill jobs, offers access to a wider set of skills, reduces headcount, and allows for more flexibility during times of change. Just like how investors have investment portfolios to diversify their holdings to mitigate risk; just like financial advisors who recommend a portfolio that consists of equities, bonds, and cash; just like executives who use the portfolio theory to analyze their business units, strategy and foresight, a career portfolio is a new way to think and talk about your professional future in order to navigate our ever-changing world of work with purpose, clarity, and flexibility.

Broadening your career focus and professional identity is no longer seen as abnormal. It is celebrated now. The macro forces driving the future of work demand independent and adaptable thinkers. With the potential for automation to transform jobs through the Great Resignation, and the growing number of hybrid offices around the world, it is clear that the time is now ripe to rethink what a successful career path looks like. Until this point, we didn't have the right words to design our careers in a way that steers away from the typical and traditional script. It used to be simple. You would start off on the lowest rung of the corporate ladder and work your way up over forty to fifty years to somewhere near the top.

What we are seeing now is a shift from pursuing a 'career path' to a 'career portfolio'. A career pathway typically tends to be a singular pursuit with slight pivots here and there, a career portfolio has the possibility of higher degree pivots incorporated into it. It represents your vast and diverse professional journey, including the twists and turns that have been made either by choice or consequence. In simpler words, it is a never-ending source of joy and fulfillment.

My portfolio, for instance, includes being an instructor in the army, being a wine promoter, a trainer's assistant, a coach, an author, a YouTuber, consultant and global speaker. Each of these identities took time for me to develop. Some of them included traditional jobs while others were pursuits of earning a part time income or plunging deep into entrepreneurship. For many individuals who are starting out in their career, a career portfolio may ease the stress and tension one would have when they think of their career pathway in a singular line of progression i.e. climbing a ladder in one direction. It is a relief to many, not just those starting out, to fully realize that your career portfolio doesn't have to be a one-size-fits-all shape. Moreover, because it is not a typical trajectory, it gives each individual more space and wisdom to try out newer things and find your own true north. Moreover, it provides multiple sources of income for the individual, which reduces risk and allows them to remove themselves from toxic environments easily. The people who endure bad leaders are usually the ones who don't really have a choice. Having a portfolio career also becomes your backup plan, just in case you lose your day job or main job. Like my Gen Z coaching client said to me, 'Being tied down is so pre-pandemic!'

The Pursuit of Polywork

The professional workforce, particularly Millennials and Gen Z, is increasingly rejecting the concept of a full-time job and a single boss in favor of what is being dubbed as 'polywork' or having multiple jobs at once. According to a study by a social network, also named Polywork, found that 55 per cent of 1000 workers it polled between twenty-one to forty years old said an exciting professional is more than just money. 64 per cent said they are already doing more than one job or hoped to in the future. More than 70 per cent surveyed believed that the pandemic has accelerated this trend. The rise of polywork dovetails with the much-documented decline in job satisfaction amidst the pandemic. Feeling undervalued, lacking communication and lacking a connection with their bosses has affected how engaged they are at their workplace. There has been a dramatic power shift from boss to talent during the pandemic. We are seeing the largest shift to entrepreneurship in history. The desire to live multifaceted lives must be understood and supported by the leaders. If businesses don't listen to their talent, we will see those companies start to become dinosaurs.[19]

Challenges You Will Face As a Leader

The gig economy is here to stay. What matters most is the way we perceive the workers who thrive with it. Most leaders may find it hard to manage a team when you don't have enough control *'over'* them. This is where the leader will need to build soft skills to establish rapport rapidly and connect with one another deeply. Building trust will no longer be based purely on having worked together, it will also be based on what type of portfolio you have. Working with bigger brands and known projects will be important for you to establish your credibility. You will also need to be able to assess whether the people you hire are the right fit for your projects. You will need to tune your skills in hiring and firing in order to find the right talents in the gig economy. Learning to look out for red flags will become a key skill to develop as the marketplace diversifies with talents across the board. On top of that, how you become a leader to people who don't report to you will be key essential skills to pick up.

---

[19] Case, Tony. 23 June 2021. 'The Job Juggle: Gen Z and Millennial Employees Embrace the Concept of 'Polywork'. *Digiday*. https://digiday.com/marketing/the-job-juggle-gen-z-and-Millennial-employees-embrace-the-concept-of-polywork/

Think about it

- Do you have a portfolio career?
- How can you create a portfolio career for yourself?
- How do you feel about hiring a gig worker?
- What are your issues with working in a gig economy?
- How will you engage strategically with the 'on-demand workforce'?
- How can they access hard-to-find expertise?
- What work can be done more successfully and efficiently by skilled gig workers?

Diversity, Equity, and Inclusion

'Diversity is having a seat at the table, inclusion is having a voice, and belonging is having that voice heard.'

—Liz and Mollie

During the World War II, the global workforce became more inclusive and diverse out of necessity. With men leaving their homes to serve in the military and demands for war material increasing, new manufacturing techniques were adopted and jobs opened up to women. Workplace diversity training first emerged in the mid-1960s, following the introduction of equal employment laws and affirmative action. Back then, companies were known for histories of racial discrimination. These new laws prompted companies to start diversity training programs that would help employees adjust to working in more integrated offices. Over time, these programs have become more elaborate and categorized into Diversity, Equity and Inclusion training. For the uninitiated, here is a simple definition of the same.

What is DEI?

When the definition of diversity is often left to personal interpretation, it becomes a problem. Without a shared understanding of inclusion, people are prone to miscommunication, progress cannot be reliably evaluated, leaders cannot be held accountable and organizations default to counting diversity numbers.

Diversity is the presence of differences that may include race, gender, generations, religion, sexual orientation, ethnicity, nationality, socioeconomic status, language, (dis)ability, religious commitment, or political perspective. Embracing diversity essentially means embracing populations that have been and remain underrepresented amongst organizations. As a leader, it means picking people from diverse backgrounds to join your team so that you get a wider spectrum of opinions instead of an echo chamber of like-minded individuals who are very similar in terms of background to you. Simply put, as my client put it, 'We want to move away from the white, pale and male' as the only description of the members in the organization.

Equity is promoting justice, impartiality, and fairness within procedures, processes, and distribution of resources by institutions or systems. Tackling equity issues requires an understanding of root causes of outcome disparities within the organization. It is about hiring a person who can speak Mandarin even if she is not Chinese. It is about ensuring there is even representation of women in the leadership team.

Inclusion is an outcome to ensure that those that are diverse actually feel welcomed. In inclusive work cultures, people feel included as they are treated equitably and with respect. Participation without favoritism is the starting point for inclusion, and this requires attention to nondiscrimination and basic courtesy. People also report feeling valued and having a sense of belonging. When people feel that their unique and authentic self is valued by others, while at the same time having a sense of connectedness or belonging to a group, they are working in inclusive cultures. Most importantly, inclusion is expressed as a safe feeling, where one can speak up safely without fear of embarrassment or retaliation, where they are empowered to grow and do one's best work. Inclusion outcomes are met when you, your organization, and your program are truly inviting to all. To the degree to which diverse individuals are able to participate fully in the decision-making processes and development opportunities within an organization. This is the by-product of doing all the right things in the right manner.[20]

---

[20] Parikh, Nish. 17 August 2021. 'Why Diversity, Equity and Inclusion Is the Need of the Hour'. *Forbes*. https://www.forbes.com/sites/forbeshumanresourcescouncil/2021/08/17/why-diversity-equity-and-inclusion-is-the-need-of-the-hour/?sh=65b16b0c7d87

Why Do Leaders Need to Know about DEI?

It is crucial for leaders to prioritize diversity now more than ever. Since the pandemic, we have seen an increase in conversations around race and racism in the workplace. With the murder of George Floyd in the US, issues around race and systemic racism were propelled to the top of the agenda by mainstream media. In a similar vein, there was a rise in anti-Asian violence in America. During this period, there has been a rise in bias, xenophobia, and racism. Employees who belong to the minorities have been looking up to their leaders in their organizations to raise awareness of the issues they have to deal with, both inside and outside the workplace. Racial discrimination against people of the Chinese heritage should warn leaders to look out for bullying, discrimination and harassment of any kind. News of these events have had its influence on organizations with a presence in Asia.[21]

Value and Belonging

Employees, especially the Millennials and the Gen Zs, expect their organization to speak out against the systemic biases in society and promise to do right by their employees. They expect leaders to be at the forefront of issues like these to be the role-model and put the spotlight on to raise awareness. Giving employees who have been marginalized an opportunity to speak and share their stories will make them feel heard and represented at the same time. This is important for employees to feel they are valued and belong with the organization. Employee health and safety must be the foremost consideration of any business as we recover from the pandemic. Understanding the needs and circumstances of employees who are diverse in all of the traditional measures but are also affected by widely varying life, work, and family conditions.

---

[21] Boston College Centre of Work & Family. (n.d.). *Covid19 Impact on Diversity and Inclusion.* https://www.bc.edu/content/dam/files/centers/cwf/research/Info%20Request_D%26IImpact_April2020.pdf

DEI is Key for Recovery

The pandemic has similarly forced us to adopt new behaviours, innovate ways of working, and challenge assumptions about who can contribute and how. This is why corporate initiatives to foster an inclusive workplace is the need of the hour that will continue to grow in the future. Previously, DEI was only considered as a 'program' to be run by companies. Now, organizations are faced with an overwhelming degree of disruption since the pandemic. DEI practices ensure that the company avoids 'groupthink' and benefits from a range of ideas, opinions and talents. The pandemic has delivered an exciting opportunity to employers to access a vastly increased talent pool. During times of uncertainty, it is important to ensure that the workplace remains inclusive. Resilience and innovation are two key qualities that characterize a diverse and inclusive organization. According to a Deloitte review in 2018, companies that follow an inclusive culture are twice more likely to meet or exceed financial targets and six times more likely to be agile and innovative. These companies are eight times more likely to achieve a better business outcome.[22]

As the world comes together to battle a deadly virus, there is a growing recognition of societal, economic, and environmental interdependencies. Such workplaces make less biased decisions and produce better ideas for solving problems. Research states that organizations that follow their diversity and inclusion policies even during a crisis are in a much better position to bounce back than their rivals that don't. It shows that diverse and inclusive teams are better at solving complex problems and make better decisions 87 per cent of the time. The need for agility and rapid innovation has led more organizations to deploy teams in which employees with diverse backgrounds collaborate to achieve short-term goals.

---

[22] Bourke, Juliet and Bernadette Dillon. 2018. 'The Diversity and Inclusion Revolution: Eight Powerful Truths'. *Deloitte Review*, no. 22 (January 2018) p. 85. https://www2.deloitte.com/content/dam/insights/us/articles/4209_Diversity-and-inclusion-revolution/DI_Diversity-and-inclusion-revolution.pdf

Organizations can no longer afford 'collections of individuals'. They must intentionally focus on unlocking the collective wisdom of teams to solve complex problems. Increasingly, people want to see the impact of their collective efforts on accelerating progressive change and driving towards a common sense of purpose of building a more sustainable and inclusive world for current and future generations. A diverse and inclusive workforce is also associated with better individual performance since employees feel motivated and engaged.[23]

Getting to this stage requires some effort from leaders. Leaders will need to overcome bias, break down siloed working practices, and build a culture of true inclusion, where everyone has a voice and feels valued for who they are. However, the actions that organizations are currently taking are still very limited in scope and ambition compared to the actions that are needed to move the needle on Diversity, Equity and Inclusion. Organizations need to switch their thought processes around DEI from risk to opportunity. Despite the widespread corporate adoption of diversity and inclusion initiatives, many organizations still struggle to provide all employees equal access to opportunities and advancement. Too often, ineffective D&I programs focus on legal compliance and risk mitigation, rather than actively understanding and promoting the rich diversity of employees. According to Korn Ferry's research, 77 per cent have developed non-discrimination, bullying and harassment policies compared to 31 per cent who have integrated DEI into business operations. These are considered baby steps because the majority are still engaged in early-stage activities such as developing DEI strategy (61 per cent) and unconscious bias training (58 per cent). Superficial diversity and inclusion programs merely mitigate legal risk, rather than uplift employees and leverage their unique perspectives. Leaders have to push their DEI efforts to the next level of maturity by embracing both structural and behavioural interventions to ensure sustainability of their efforts.

---

[23] Ibid. https://www2.deloitte.com/content/dam/insights/us/articles/4209_Diversity-and-inclusion-revolution/DI_Diversity-and-inclusion-revolution.pdf

A few ways to move the needle include:

Develop Inclusive Leaders at Every Level

Inclusive leaders embrace the full diversity of today's workforces and know how to create a safe space where people feel accepted and empowered to give their best. They are critical for enabling effective collaboration but are also extremely rare. According to Korn Ferry's report, only 5 per cent of leaders are inclusive. Organizations can better develop inclusive leaders by providing more training on this topic.

Hold Leaders Accountable

According to Korn Ferry's research, only one in four organizations have DEI KPIs in place for people managers. This needs to change. One of the most effective ways to incorporate DEI with talent management is to hold leaders accountable for it.

Build DEI into the Fabric of the Organization

Tackling individual biases is an important step on the way to creating a diverse and inclusive organization. But more needs to be done. For the behavioural changes to stick, it is critical to implement structural inclusion as well. This means re-examining of organizational structures, processes, practices, and algorithms to remove systemic biases and ensure equity for all. This means leaders need to be involved in designing systems around the needs of the most underrepresented employee to make them better for everybody.

Make DEI Part of How You Innovate

Companies with above-average diversity report 19 per cent higher innovation revenue. To boost collective intelligence and problem-solving, start deploying diverse-by-design teams, particularly in areas such as R&D, marketing, and customer services.

Companies like Microsoft, Google, Adobe, and Nike are driving innovation and better products through the application of inclusive design. They co-design with people who have a diversity of perspective, including those that can't use or have difficulty using the current design. Nike developed its famous shoes without shoelaces for those who had cerebral palsy but many other customers, including children and pregnant women, enjoyed the outcomes of it.[24]

Copy and Paste Strategies from the West won't Work

This is a common mistake leaders make in Asia. Merely copy-pasting the same DEI approach that worked in the West will not work out in the East for obvious cultural reasons. Asking people to share their vulnerabilities openly in a room full of people, where your colleagues and especially your boss is in, goes against the cultural norms we have been brought up in. In Asia, we have been rewarded for obedience and deference to authority and even giving suggestions when your boss is angry can be misconstrued as being defiant. There is no long tradition of challenging norms or open debates. Just take a look at our history of 'Asian parenting values' that prize obedience and putting the collective over the individual. Even our schools still assess students based on unyielding rubrics with little space for divergent and free thinking. As much as I would like to think we have improved from how it used to be, we still are a long way from speaking out in a public setting on issues that have been conversed privately for decades. Approaches like these can backfire and might actually make people feel disconnected, anxious, resentful and unsafe. Asia needs a subtler approach and drilling down on the concept of psychological safety is the first step to getting Asian employees to speak up without fear of repercussions.

Forcing People with 'Rules' might Create the Unintended Effect

In the story 'Hidden Figures' by Margot Lee Shetterly, a character by the name Dorothy Vaughan moves from her hometown in Newport to work at the Langley Memorial Aeronautical Laboratory. This is happening

---

[24]Korn Ferry. (n.d.). *Future of Work Trends 2022.* https://www.kornferry.com/content/dam/kornferry-v2/featured-topics/pdf/FOW_TrendsReport_2022.pdf

in the 1960s, and her experience of traveling in a bus from home to get to work is a rather unique one. The rules around transportation at that time was such that the front door of the bus was used by the white people to enter and exit, while the back door by the black people. In fact, there even was a coloured line in the middle of the bus that divided the bus into two sections to maintain this deliberate segregation. This was a rule that everyone adhered to back then, when diversity and inclusion wasn't even a thing. So sometimes, when the front section was really full, the black people had to give up seats for white people. The challenge was, in many cases, there was a shortage of bus conductors. You have to understand, technology was not advanced back then. People had to get their bus tickets from bus conductors. Therefore, when the buses ran with a limited number of bus conductors, it meant that there was no one manning the back door of the bus. Black people had no choice but to enter through the front door and they had to make their way to the back of the bus by moving through the confined space of the bus, which was already filled with people. Sometimes, due to the chaos and traffic, a lot of the white people would find themselves in the back of the bus and they would have to do the same thing—jostle their way to the front section where they belong. After traveling in the bus for a number of times, Dorothy observes that, '. . . if the segregation laws were designed to reduce friction by keeping the races apart, in practice, they had the complete opposite effect.'

The same happens in the workforce. When we copy and paste rules, guidelines and policies without customizing it for our organizational culture, we end up in a place where they actually have the complete opposite effects. To make matters worse, many training efforts we have seen in Asia tend to be 'cut and paste' from US unconscious bias training programmes and rolled out globally, featuring content mainly about 'blacks vs whites', and aimed at redressing historical injustices such as slavery and racial equity. This turns off audiences in Asia, who ironically feel a sense of cultural insensitivity and lack of relevance to their context. Force-feeding and clumsy training efforts can actually make things worse, and lead to the 'backfire effect' as it is called in psychology, where employees become resentful and more convinced of their own beliefs when presented with opposing evidence.

Challenges You Will Face as a Leader

As a leader, you will be forced to face your own demons first. Identifying your own biases, and realizing you aren't as perfect as you would like to seem in front of your team, may be unsettling at first. But take heart, that is the first step. As organizations around the world embrace diversity, equity, and inclusion, more individuals will have the ability to look inwards and identify their biases and how to deal with them. Being able to take this step earlier will give you an added advantage of having difficult conversations around sensitive topics like bias with your team members. It will be hard, but it will also empower you to be more sensitive to issues that other minorities working under you face. Most importantly, it will make you a better leader, even if you don't know all the answers. Being willing to step into this space, unlearn the bad practices, and pick up the best practices, will ensure you stand out as a leader in any organization. The biggest missing piece in this is leadership. We have yet to see leaders modeling the behaviour they want to see, rather than just checking the box by asking HR to organize unconscious bias programs which tend to be useless in establishing behaviour change. Asians are skeptical by nature, and will need to see leaders sharing their own stories of bias and admitting their own mistakes and unconscious biases. Only when you praise your team members for speaking up, will you see the people you lead experience a higher level of psychological safety and trust with you.

Think about it

- Do you have the psychological safety within your organization and with your boss to speak out on issues that are difficult to discuss?
- Have you had to speak about diversity, equity or inclusion to your boss or colleague before?
- Have you made it clear to your team members that they can approach you openly if they are facing some issues?
- Have you seen or experienced leaders throwing such topics under the carpet because they thought it wasn't important?

- Have you attended any training on diversity, equity, and inclusion to better deal with difficult issues at the workplace?
- Do your team members feel a sense of psychological safety around you and come to you with their problems?
- How will you deal with a team member who is feeling ostracized at work because of their race, religion, sexual orientation, gender, generation or nationality?
- Have you been given the required training of proper facilitation skills to tackle 'difficult conversations' around diversity and inclusion?

Leading Across Generations

We need to remember across generations that there is much to learn as much as there is to teach.

—Gloria Steinem

To lead across generations, one must know the different generations that exist. Here is a breakdown of the different generations.

Name	Year	Age in 2020
The Traditionalists	1925–1945	75–95
Baby Boomers	1946–1964	56–74
Generation X	1965–1979	41–55
Millennials	1980–1995	25–40
Generation Z	1996–2010	10–24
Gen Alpha	2011–	0–9

Why would leading across generations be a new thing? The workforce has always had a multigenerational workforce. The multigenerational workforce has always had members of different generations ever since the generational labels were introduced. So you might be wondering, what is so different about this particular instance? We have always had a workforce with multiple generations working in it. Well, I'm glad you asked.

For a long time, the younger generations have always worked under the older generations. Senior positions were awarded to seniors who had accumulated the relevant experiences over time. Hence, the longer you have been in the workforce, you are perceived as being more senior and capable. However, as technology accelerates at unimaginable speeds, the older generations are finding it harder to keep up with the changes that are happening in the working world. This is where Millennials are stepping up to occupy leadership positions. Hence, leading across generations for the Millennial leader would mean managing team members who are senior in age and experience as well as juniors who are much more exposed and in tune with technology. Leading across generations comes with a unique twist for Millennials as people of all ages will follow a leader based on their competencies that may not necessarily be tagged to their age. In a post-pandemic era, it will not be surprising for Millennials to be leading team members consisting of full-time and part-time staff with ages ranging between twenty-two and seventy-two.

How Generations Got Their Names

The Baby Boomers got their name after the baby boom that happened globally and was used to refer to those born during the boom after the Second World War. The Gen Xers were named Gen X because they didn't really have much in common globally. Millennials (also known as Generation Y) was the name coined in 1991 by Neil Howe and William Strauss in their book *Generations.* Initially, the name was Generation Y, which was then changed to Millennials as this generation hit the millennium (year 2000) in their developing years. Gen Z, as you can easily presume, is the name of the next generation, following the alphabetical order. It is possible that this generation gets named the 'Coronials', given that the coronavirus is one of the biggest events that has happened during their developing years. The Traditionalists have retired and are not as active in the workforce today. However, the remaining four generations from Baby Boomers to Gen Z will have the opportunity to work together.

Baby Boomers are Not Retiring from Work

According to the Kelly Global Workforce Index Survey of over 164,000 workers from over twenty-eight countries, a shift we are noticing is that Baby Boomers are not retiring from work and are willing to pursue alternative working arrangements in later life, even possibly have second or third careers. With the global life expectancy of humans rising from thirty-one in 1900s to seventy-one in 2015 and with technology and medicine continuing to advance, the first person to live up to 150 has likely already been born. With the gig economy allowing more individuals to work freely with different organizations, Baby Boomers are keeping themselves occupied post retirement by joining organizations that accept seniors into the workforce. As skilled candidates come in short supply in almost every industry across the globe, the competition for talent is intense. Savvy employers today are the ones creating a diverse workforce of people of all ages and adapting their recruitment, retention, retirement and other workforce strategies to accommodate the needs of all generations. This allows them to maintain their organization's institutional and market knowledge, mitigate labor shortages, and unlock new sources of competitive advantage.

Gen Zs Are Joining the Workforce Earlier

Gen Zs don't believe in education the same way as the generations before them do, and are joining the workforce at a much earlier age. Baby Boomers viewed education as a dream, Gen Xers saw it as a differentiator, Millennials embraced it as a cultural norm, and Gen Zers saw it as a need for law and medical students only. Baby Boomers held education to such a high regard because it was a key differentiator in those times. However, times have changed and many argue that the only reason college remains relevant today is due to societal and peer pressure. To many Baby Boomers and Gen Xers, they failed as a parent if their child didn't qualify to go to college and attain a graduate degree. So getting a college degree seems to be more of a social norm than a smart career move.

According to Larry Summers, an economist at Harvard University, not enough people are innovating enough in higher education. Organizations like General Electric look nothing like it looked in 1975, but educational institutions like Harvard, Yale, and Princeton look pretty similar to what they looked like in 1975. For an industry like education, that is all about ideas and innovation, the rate of change of improvement is stunningly slow. Hence, the relevance of higher education is becoming questionable to a generation that has information readily available 24/7 at the swipe of a finger. 75 per cent of Gen Zers are saying that there are other ways of getting a good education than going to college.[25]

Gen Z is seriously considering forgoing a traditional college education to go work in a company that provides college-like training. This is because companies too are providing such opportunities as a more effective way to recruit and retain top talents. According to Jenn Prevoznik, the Global Head of Early Talent Acquisition from SAP, she is fully supportive of Gen Zers skipping college to come work for SAP because what really matters are their skills and not necessarily their degree. In Germany and Bangalore, SAP brings university education to their employees. On the weekends, professors come to SAP buildings and teach full-time employees. Gen Z students are now asking corporations if they will help them get new skills as jobs shift. According to a Dell Technologies prediction, 85 per cent of the jobs that will exist in 2030 haven't been invented yet. Hence, Gen Zers are asking the very pertinent question, 'How will a four-year degree sustain me for my 100+ year career in a high-flux world?' Front-loading on education for a few years is no longer an accurate marker of one's strengths and talents in the working world.

According to Inc., 61 per cent of Gen Z who are still in high school and 43 per cent of Gen Z who are in college say they would rather be

[25] Jenkins, Ryan. 19 July 2017. 'Generation Z versus Millenials: The 8 Differences You Need to Know'. *Inc.* https://www.inc.com/ryan-jenkins/generation-z-vs-millennials-the-8-differences-you-.html

entrepreneurs than employees when they graduate. The gig economy has made this all the more possible as the online world evolves into a marketplace for many people to buy and sell.[26] Lastly, Gen Zers are starting to question the value of the college certificate given the cost of the degree. Since 1978, the cost of the college degree has increased 151.1 per cent while the median income has only increased about 20.2 per cent. Naturally, we see a 74 per cent increase in student debt because of the exorbitant costs of outdated education. Even for Gen Z in Asia, where parents are known to pay off the cost of college, this is a sum that doesn't add up. In fact, Gen Zers see this as a debt that can be easily avoided by starting to go to work earlier.[27]

Intergenerational diversity is diversity and is a highly important and universal fact in the sustainability and prosperity of today's work environment. Great leaders don't only have a profound understanding of the differences among generations, they also recognize the importance of putting those differences to work in finding more creative solutions to problems. They are adept at fostering robust, productive dialog and engaging team members in giving their highest and best contributions. Understanding the difference of values between these generational groups can help visionary leaders, managers, and supervisors build on the strengths of such diversity and create an organizational culture that embraces coexistence, cooperation, and teamwork. No one generation can make it alone.

Challenges You Will Face as a Leader

As a Millennial leader, it is important to understand what motivates your team members. Developing an understanding and appreciation of how generations differ can help you create higher-functioning

[26] White, John. 11 September 2017. 'Learn Why Top Gen Zers Are Skipping Schools to Become Entrepreneurs'. *Inc.* https://www.inc.com/john-white/learn-why-top-gen-zers-are-skipping-school-to-beco.html?cid=nl029week37day12

[27] Jenkins, Ryan. 'This is Why Generation Z Will Skip College'. Blog. https://blog.ryan-jenkins.com/this-is-why-generation-z-will-skip-college

teams and a more satisfying environment as it helps you address natural points of tension that emerge because of those differences. Not knowing these key points of differences amongst the generations will only undermine your efforts as a leader to do the right thing for the right employee from the respective generation. A one-size-fits-all blanket approach will not work to engage your team members like it used to. Most leaders are empathetic but don't appear empathetic, and that's the reason they find leadership a struggle. Most don't even fully understand the concept of empathy.

Empathy is not the ability to take on another person's feelings. Empathy is the ability to describe another person's perspective and feelings back to them.

More often than not, many conflicts that happen at the workplace, happen due to unexplained expectations. The older generations grew up in different times and their mindset has mostly been shaped by the experiences they had when they were younger. Their expectations at work are based on these 'reference experiences'. The younger generations, in the same vein, have grown up in a world that is completely different from the world the older generations lived in. Their expectations and experiences are way different. Social, economic, and technological advances have widened the generational gap today. Yes, that means you have to really dive deeper into what is important for the individual from different generations. Having deeper heart-to-heart conversations with your employees will help you understand what matters most to them. Understanding the generations empowers you as the leader to identify patterns and be on the safer side. Getting to know each team member on an individual level will help provide more insight on how to bring out the best in them. The challenge remains in organizing all of this information and keeping track and remembering the details with each individual. It is almost as if you need to have a rolodex to store information for each individual. Having a notebook to store key information of your team members to remember simple things like their favorite food, big dream, bucketlist ideas are all simple yet powerful ways to deepen relationships with your team members.

Think about it

- Do you face any challenges working with individuals from different generations?
- Have you experienced 'unexplained expectations' when communicating with colleagues from different generations?
- Do you notice conflicts amongst team members from different generations?
- Have you felt that your team is not aligned due to a generational gap?
- Have you noticed any generational stereotypes play out during team conversations amongst your team members?
- Do team members tend to form cliques based on their age?
- Do you find it hard to please all team members from different generations in your team?
- Are you currently aware of what is on the bucket list of your team members?
- Are you keeping track of the dreams and aspirations of your team members?
- In which areas do you struggle the most in managing your team members—motivation, communication, work ethics, or something else?

Whether you are a leader in a global corporation or running a small team in a startup, your role is to bring their brains to work and collaborate with each other to solve problems and accomplish work that's perpetually changing. Leaders must find and keep on finding new ways to create value to thrive over the long term by putting the talents you have to its best and highest use. Few leaders actually stop to think about the implications of the new reality and what it means for the kind of work environment that would help their team members thrive and succeed. To complicate matters, as companies become increasingly complex and global in the post-pandemic, more and more of the work is team based. Employees at all levels are spending 50 per cent more time collaborating than they did twenty years ago.[28]

Most work requires people to talk to each other to sort out changing interdependencies. Based on the constant changes from the pandemic as well as the upcoming trends that are to be expected from all the changes we are seeing around us, it is pretty clear that Millennial leaders will need to develop deeper human skills that will empower them to manage their intergenerational teams effectively. The goal of the next part of this book is to help you do just that, and to equip you with some new ideas and practices to make your job easier. In the chapters that follow, I will be covering why Millennials are wired differently and the key areas to work on to lead an intergenerational team effectively in a new normal.

---

[28] Cross, Rob, Reb Rebele, and Adam Grant. 'Collaborative Overload'. *Harvard Business Review* (January–February 2016). https://hbr.org/2016/01/collaborative-overload

Chapter 4: Why Millennials Are Wired Differently

'Millennials', 'Gen Y', and 'The Peter Pan Generation' are the many names that Millennials go by. One cannot hear the word 'Millennial' without a swarm of preconceived notions filling the mind. While this remains true for all generations, the situation is pretty egregious for the Millennial generation. Even though Baby Boomers and Gen Xers also face their fair share of stereotypes, they have not received the same level of attention as the Millennials. One cannot talk about the importance of harmonizing the generations at work without fully understanding the impact that the Millennial generation brings to the workforce.

Millennials are now the largest adult cohort worldwide and also the most educated and they have a strong influence on society. Today, there are 1.8 billion Millennials worldwide which equals 23 per cent of the global population. In Asia alone, we have 1.1 billion Millennials which accounts for the highest concentration of these Millennials. Millennials and Gen Z are projected to make up 75 per cent of the Association of Southeast Asian Nations (ASEAN) consumers by 2030.[29] Undoubtedly, as a leader, you will oversee fellow Millennials at some

---

[29] Neufeld, Dorothy. 8 November 2021. 'There are 1.8 Billion Millennials on Earth. Here's Where They Live'. *World Economic Forum*. https://www.weforum.org/agenda/2021/11/millennials-world-regional-breakdown/#:~:text=Asia%20is%20unmatched%20when%20it,thirds%20of%20the%20country's%20passports

point in your career. In this chapter, I will help you understand the driving forces, strengths, and liabilities of this generation so that you can work with them better. Secondly, I will also share with you how other generations view our generation and how you can successfully bridge the gap.

If you've been in the workforce long enough, or if you are a Millennial yourself, you probably have likely been bombarded with literature on Millennials and feel like you've heard enough. However, in order to look forward, it is imperative we take a step back and look at the changes this generation has brought about, the changes that we have benefited from and how this generation is paving the way for Gen Z to achieve even more meaningful things.

This generation forced the world to realize one thing: the voice of the youth matters. They do have valuable and important things to say, they can and should contribute, they can achieve great things and build strong companies, and their voice should be heard. Prior to this generation, the common understanding was that youths were empty containers, treated like recruits with no rank and no value, with a lot of space to be filled by people with experience. They only held any value once they became fully indoctrinated by older generations or after developing enough expertise on their own. Sadly, in many companies, this is the state of affairs where respect is only given when you have achieved something worthy of mention or if you have been working in the organization long enough to be called a senior employee. If this is the case for the Millennial generation, you can only imagine how bad it was for the Gen Xers, Baby Boomers, and Traditionalists.

This generation is the one that decided to put an end to the old way of working brought about by the industrial revolution. They pushed for better workplaces to avoid becoming a corporate zombie themselves where they work in cookie cutter cubicles while hiding their passions and personality. They stopped thinking twice before letting go of the toxic boss they have been working under in a moment's notice and spend their life in hope of finally being able to do all the things they always dreamed of without having to retire. They believe in experiencing life in the present and live by the

YOLO phrase—you only live once—which gives them the strength and conviction to pursue alternatives to a typical, proper job. The pandemic has given them enough time to pause and rethink their decisions around their career. In America alone, 4.5 million people have resigned from their organization over the past two years and they continue to exit in a mass exodus. In this exodus, Millennials are seen as the most likely to take flight. Why are Millennials wired this way? What led them to have such distinctive characteristics? Are these merely stereotypes or is there any truth to what you read about this generation? We uncover the truths in this chapter.

As a Millennial, you probably know most of the things I'm going to share with you here anyway. However, for those of you who have not read up any literature on this generation, it will help you understand this generation from a different vantage point. Having this understanding is critical to leading this generation. Of course, this chapter is only a snapshot. If you would like to dive deeper into understanding the Millennial generation, do check out my book *Engaging Millennials*. First, let's take a look at the key forces that shaped some of the common characteristics associated with this generation.

Financial

Millennials have borne the brunt of three financial crises in their growing years. The first one in 1997, also known as the Asian Financial Crisis. Wave 1 Millennials born in the 1980s were in their early teens when this event happened. They felt the effect it had on their families and how it affected the opportunities they had in the job market. The second Lehmann-brothers crisis happened in 2008, where Millennials born in the late 80s and early 90s were in their teens. Even during this time, Millennials saw their parents struggle with fears of being retrenched despite their many years of loyal service. Lastly, we have the COVID-19 crisis which greatly impacts the youngest of the Millennials and oldest of Gen Zs born in the late 90s. The repercussions of the economy have shaped the decision-making process with Millennials. As this generation grew up, they noticed the disconnect between the loyalty their parents showed and the loyalty the organizations showed in return. It became pretty clear to them that in times of crises, organizations focus on staying afloat by cutting down on talent. Loyalty from the management's point of view is not towards the employee, but rather the shareholder.

This made it really difficult for them to justify staying in an organization till retirement for the golden watch, long service award and certificate of loyalty. They realized that it is the system that is wrecked; too many companies have been taking advantage of employees for far too long. Which is why even in this day and age, when you ask people, 'How's work?', the most typical response you get is 'It's fine'. Rarely do we see anyone say, 'I'm loving it here' or 'It's been really great, I really enjoy the work I'm doing right now and I'm learning a lot'. Prior to COVID-19, the unknown was scarier than staying in a bad job. However, with COVID-19, people realized that quitting the unknown is not as scary as it seemed to be. A lot of people had their incomes shaken and strained, and yet, they survived. Hence all of a sudden, the complications or the narrative that we tell ourselves about the unknown were not as scary anymore. Hence, now when we compare 'fine' with the 'unknown', a lot of people are a lot less afraid of the unknown.

The Great Resignation that we are dealing with is actually the breaking point of years and years and years of mistreatment by companies who got away with mediocre corporate cultures. The financial crises are always a time of complete upheaval where the old gets flushed out to make way for the new. Millennials have had three financial crises to brave through and it has no doubt made an impact in the way Millennials think about loyalty towards an organization. Here's a speech by Pete Davis, who gave it a name.

'It's late at night and you start browsing Netflix looking for something to watch. You scroll through different titles, you even read a few reviews, but you just can't commit to watching any given movie. Suddenly, it's been 30 minutes and you're still stuck in infinite browsing mode. So, you just give up. You're too tired to watch anything now. So you cut your losses and fall asleep. I've come to believe that this is the defining characteristic of our generation. Let's call it "keeping our options open".'

Social

Baby Boomers took an active role in being a parent. They wanted to provide the best life for their children, and they went out of their way to ensure it. Baby Boomers were raised by strict and conservative parents who believed in an authoritarian approach more than a democratic one. Times were harsh back then, where basic food, water, shelter and more were the biggest priorities for them. There was a clear hierarchy in the house, with the father being the head of the household, followed by the mother being the second-in-chief and the oldest son or daughter as the next in power. As parents, Baby Boomers decided to be a lot more diplomatic with their children. They ensured their children had everything they wanted and were more liberal in their approach. They became the biggest cheerleader and supporter and this had a strong impact on the mindset Millennials have today. Parents spend a lot of time being very concerned about other parents who aren't involved enough in the lives of their children and their upbringing. It came to a point where they started feeling their child could not be successful unless they were there to protect their children.

As a result, Millennials became accustomed to having adult figures helping them out at every nook and corner of their journey. It became a checklisted childhood, and with the over-help, parents deprived their children from building self-efficacy. Self-efficacy is built when one sees that one's own actions leads to outcomes. As a result, the Millennial generation was quickly labeled 'entitled' because of the needs they expressed to their managers. The amount of handholding they expected came across as a cultural shock for many Baby Boomer and Gen X managers, who were thrown in the waters and told to learn to swim by themselves. Millennials, on the other hand, preferred a leader who would acknowledge their efforts and appreciate the work they have been doing. They sought for constant feedback and relied on their leaders to know that they were directionally correct. Affirmations became important for this generation and they looked up to their leaders for it, and they learnt this behaviour from their parents, school guidance counselors and educators who have gone out of their way to help Millennials in their pursuit of success. All of the support and guidance from adult figures have shaped Millennials to be much more outspoken in the workplace. Senior managers have also commented that Millennials do not take criticism well and some have even used labels such as 'snowflakes' and 'strawberries' to describe their younger counterparts. A lot of the behaviours that Millennials displayed were frowned upon by managers even though by large, it is not their fault. They were raised in different times and in different parenting styles and hence, they developed different expectations of their managers and the workplace that they want to belong to. Millennials by and large do not subscribe to the notion of tolerating toxic workplaces and think of wearing it as a badge of honor. Surviving toxic workplaces will inevitably build resilience, but it is considered a waste of time and energy when they were inundated with so many income opportunities that the internet brought along.

Technological

Another key trend that is worth mentioning is the rise of technology as Millennials were growing up. This generation experienced life before the internet as well the one after it. Technology was a source of inspiration to many as it unleashed so many possibilities. It was impossible to think that one could communicate to hundreds of people through a video call while working at home back in the '90s. The internet was the up-and-coming new kid on the block and Millennials were very involved in using it to connect with their peers. Technology offered convenience and instilled the mindset of efficiency amongst this generation. Technology evolved so fast that it created an 'upgrade cycle' mindset amongst the youths to have the same kind of progress in their lives. They judged their lives based on the highlight reels that others put out on social media and it affected their self-esteem in a negative manner. The smartphone changed everything and made social media erupt. Instant messaging became popular and interacting with peers on a digital front became the thing everyone was talking about. Gaming became popular as they collaborated in teams to achieve a common objective. Evolving technology vastly expanded choice. As a result, Millennials became really savvy with technology. They understood it a little better and didn't fear making mistakes on it. Social media made it even more complex as this generation started comparing themselves with their peers. As a result, this generation grew up to be much more tech-savvy than people-savvy. Their comfort levels of communication leans towards texting as opposed to having in-person conversations. The notifications that they get from their devices have had them hooked on it just like many people are addicted to alcohol and nicotine. Being on social media has also created an alternate form of communication where memes are made in context to the world they are familiar with. Millennials even created their own slang as they communicated through online communities. All in all, technology played a critical role in shaping the Millennials and the mindset they have today.

Unique Characteristics of This Generation

Tech-savvy

There is no doubt that the majority of the Millennial generation are more tech-savvy than other generations before them. Millennials grew up in a time of the digital revolution. Mobile phones became smart phones in a matter of years. Google became a verb that is used commonly in daily conversations and like it or not, Millennials are always seen with their phones. Millennials can do a lot more with their phones than their parents, who use it primarily for texting and calling. Millennials use their smartphones to read reviews, book flights or movie tickets, purchase items online, stay connected with their friends, send emails, navigate new places with Google maps, take notes, create and edit video content to upload on social media and even book a cab. They can leave home without their wallet but they absolutely cannot exist without their phones with which they manage their lives. It is no surprise that Millennials are always seen with their heads down, looking at their phones even in a room full of people as they wait for the meeting to start. Technology has empowered us, and it has also disabled us in many ways.

What This Means for You

As a Millennial leader, it is easier for you to understand why Millennials treasure their phone and use it so much. Sometimes, it is too much, but that is because technology has empowered us to do many things with this simple device in our hands. It means you will need to be a lot more patient with Millennials and Gen Zs for constantly using their phone even when you are talking to them and you will have to employ even more patience with the older generation who are not as tech-savvy, which means you will have to slow down to guide them with the technology. It can be frustrating to be bridging the divide, but this is the challenge you will have to conquer in order to build a strong team. If so much can be done with technology, how can you leverage your Millennial and even Gen Z team members to get more done with technology? How can you get your Baby Boomer and Gen X employees to be even more tech-savvy and not have any fears with regards to technology?

How can you ensure your company and team stay up-to-date technologically? Knowing that Millennials are tech-savvy also means they will be excited to test out new softwares and push the boundaries to what technology can do to make things even more efficient. Millennials are always in *beta mode,* i.e., they are always improving and testing things out. This is a mindset that has been ingrained in them because they grew up with technology constantly evolving in a short period of time. It also means that they will loathe outdated, old-school systems and processes for something that can be automated with technology. Not only will it waste time, it will generate lots of frustrations if something that can be completed in two steps with technology takes ten minutes manually. Being tech-savvy has its pros and cons, but instead of seeing this as only a bad thing, it will be much more powerful if you fully unleash the potential of your tech-savvy employees to test new boundaries.

Multitaskers

Millennials are known to multitask, even though many scientists believe that multi-tasking itself is a myth. What we actually do is 'switch-task' very quickly. However, because we are so bombarded by notifications right, left and center, we keep on switching from one task to the other very fast. Unfortunately or fortunately, Millennials have become really good at switching tasks just the way flies sit on something for a while and then move on to the next. We learnt this from young, where we headed off to complete another task as the computer downloaded and installed the latest updates. Except, now, we do it without phones. You're probably guilty of it yourself, where you send out emails as you queue up for food, while also chatting with your colleagues on WhatsApp and also making bank transfers with your phone. I know I am, and I'm not even apologetic about it. There is just so much that we can do with technology and many are proud of even the few seconds that we shave off with multitasking. Millennials have been trained to be efficient and technology reinforces this. It is all about speed and ticking things off the to-do list as fast as possible, especially if it can be done faster with technology.

What This Means for You

You sit down at your desk to work on an important project, but a notification pops up. Later, as you attempt to get back into work, a colleague taps your shoulder to check on something. Then, as you try to go back to start on your project, your colleague from another department asks you what you're planning to have for lunch and you get distracted again. This is the reality of many individuals at work, and it has become really hard for many to put our devices down to focus. This is because our personal and professional lives have become strongly intertwined with a device that delivers both types of notifications. As a Millennial leader, you will have to set the stage right by being the role model. This means you must become 'indistractable' and have high levels of focus and output. Then, and only then, can you strive to influence your team members who are constantly task-switching. In order to bring some calm into the chaos, you will need to set your expectations right from the beginning. If your Millennial employees have deadlines to meet, you will be less likely to find them surfing social media on their phones when they are in the office. You can also set up expectations on when it is okay for them to be multitasking, and when you really need them to be 'all hands on deck'. Having clear expectations reduces ambiguity and strengthens the culture of the team as everyone follows suit. Additionally, you will also have to guide your team members to build upon their ability to focus. In his book *Indistractable*, Nir Eyal recommends his readers to take up the challenge of doing a single task without entertaining any distractions. If that means putting your phone away until that task is complete, do it. If it means you book a separate booth to get work done, do it. When your team can see the clear-cut benefits of being indistractable, they too will follow your lead.

Digitally Connected

When the internet came along, everyone was given a dais and a microphone but no one was formally taught on how to use them. It took some time for the older generations to realize the power of technology. The fact that the internet could change the way we communicate, shop, and entertain ourselves was seen as a surprise to many from the older generations. It took some time for them to completely trust the internet. Whereas the Millennials, who grew up during the time when such advances were being made, caught on to the power of technology that was made available to the individual. Social media has allowed us to have over 5000 friends on Facebook, 30,000 connections on LinkedIn, and unlimited followers on Instagram and TikTok. We have the power to reach out to people in an instant. We can look up the people we are about to meet before we meet them. We can see what they have been up to with the help of social media. We can customize our approaches to engage with them based on what we can find out about them online. Millennials are known to spend their free time on social media, simply browsing through content from our friends, families and followers. It also allows for a free flow of information. If the company has new announcements to make, it will reach Millennials much faster if you put it up on the company's social media platforms compared to sending it through the intranet platforms. That is how fast information travels on social media. Being digitally connected also means there are a variety of ways we can communicate. We can text, send voice messages, do video calls, send emails and many more these days. What's more, each of us have different expectations and instincts about whether it is appropriate to send a text or an email, when to look into the camera during a video call, how long to wait before we write back to someone, how to write a digital thank you note or apology without appearing sloppy or insincere. Our word choices, response times, video meeting styles, email sign-offs, and even our email signatures can create impressions that can either enhance or wreck our closest relationships at the workplace.

What This Means for You

A study by Annalise Knudson, who studied teens to see if they prefer texting to talking, found out that 25 per cent of respondents socialize more frequently online than in person. A 2015 Pew survey found that 90 per cent of cell phone owners 'frequently' carry their phones with them, with 76 per cent admitting they turn off their phones 'rarely' or 'never'. Like it or not, Millennials will continue to use social media for personal and professional purposes. What you want to establish early on with your team are your thoughts around privacy. Do you want to be connected with your work colleagues, or do you want to keep it purely professional? Millennials tend to engage with leaders who are much more fun to be around. In other words, they like the element of play to be incorporated with work. This means you do not treat them formally like how the Gen X or Baby Boomer bosses would. Being more like them, you must learn to incorporate both. Being connected with them socially means you get to peek into their personal lives and they get to do the same. It means they can connect with other individuals from the same organization and also build stronger working relationships across departments. It means that information will be easily available for them and they are able to become really resourceful to get things done. It also means you might find out they don't just work with you as a full-time employee, they also have many other sources of income generation thanks to the internet. On the other hand, it also means that this generation and the Gen Zs, for that matter, will struggle more with having deep and serious conversations. Even our traditional body language patterns have shifted thanks to our devices. When one person is leading the team meeting, many others can be seen stealing glances at their phones to handle other 'urgent' matters. This also happens in business lunches and I'm pretty sure the same habits repeat back home.

While it is easy to like and comment on one's social media post, it is a completely different ballgame to sit down and have heart-to-heart conversations with someone in person. Having the right communication skills such as identifying important non-verbal cues, reading facial micro expressions, and distinguishing the difference in vocal intonations will be something they will need more help with. According to psychologist Daniel Goleman, famous for his work on Emotional Intelligence, reading emotions within the digital nature of the modern workplace has become a new challenge, especially for leaders. The loss of nonverbal cues is among one of the most overlooked reasons why employees are feeling so disengaged with one another. Disengagement is happening not because employees don't want to be engaged, but rather, because they don't know how to engage given the tools they have today. We are cue-less today. We are growing more accepting of distractions and indifferent to the needs and emotions of our colleagues. So even if we are digitally well-connected, we are at the same time, digitally disconnected. Our timing is off with digital communication. If we were having a conversation standing next to each other, we would have immediate responses. However, any urgent texts that have been sent may take hours to get a response just because it either got buried under the many texts or it was conveniently ignored by the receiver. Today, we are no longer obliged to respond to someone immediately and this often leaves the other party feeling anxious or resentful.

Instant Gratification and Recognition

One of the by-products of being accustomed to convenience is the expectation of instant gratification. Over the years, technology developed at supersonic speeds and allowed for a high level of convenience. It shaped the way we consume food, travel, and seek entertainment. Raise your hand if you've ever felt a tinge of irritation when a website takes longer to load than it usually does. We are all victims of this, and it takes conscious effort to remove ourselves from these dire consequences. After talking to some Millennials, I have even learnt that some of them experience anxiety when someone has seen their WhatsApp message, blue ticked them, and not yet responded. The anxiety comes from their inability to wait for a response, especially when someone has already read the message that was sent out. This is a cause for concern and the only way we can overcome this is by practicing patience. I talk to so many smart, fantastic, ambitious, idealistic, hardworking young individuals, who are right out of college or in entry level jobs, who say they're going to quit their jobs because they are not making a big enough impact. They treat fulfillment like a scavenger hunt, something that they should look for constantly and they sift through multiple jobs because they're not finding what they are always looking for. This entire generation has institutionalized a sense of impatience. They struggle to go on a journey that might take longer than they expect and talk themselves down when they see their peers reporting their milestone wins on social media. Instant success and instant results have become the mantra that many are focused on, without realizing the amount of hard work and effort they need to put in to get to their desired level of success.

This goes for career advancement in particular, as Millennials are touted to be job hoppers because we have realized that if the only way up is out, then we're out. Many managers have repeatedly mentioned that this generation tends to want to move up the ladder really quickly without having put in the work. They tend to desire before they deserve and it becomes frustrating when they leave even when they don't have the merit to move up. The expectations that they have about advancing in their careers come from the upgrade cycle as mentioned above. It is gleaned from our environment where we are constantly observing how things are moving really fast in our industry to how many of our peers are climbing the ladders and sharing them on social media. It builds a narrative in one's head to start picking up the pace faster in order to keep up. The fear of missing out is real and it affects this generation in many ways so leaders will need to know how they can set the expectations right for them and pace them well so that they make the most of their career.

What This Means for You

Patience is a virtue, and it is something that we will need to consciously incorporate into our lives by being mindful of our internal reactions when things don't operate at the optimum speeds that we have been conditioned to. There is a famous quote on patience that I believe will shed great light into this.

'Patience is not simply the ability to wait but rather the attitude we adopt while we are waiting.'

—Joyce Meyer

Sharing stories of your own career journey can be a huge inspiration to others who are new to the organization or industry. It is one of the best ways to share a powerful lesson without being preachy about it. In this case, sharing the merits of being patient can help the impatient individuals in your team to reconsider their decision to move out. Of course, many leaders in the past led the way with empty promises and this is something everyone should avoid. Empty promises will wear out the trust the individual has in the leader and it will only serve to make them find greener pastures faster. Success is a long journey and if you can map out the milestones that come between where your team members are at currently to where they want to go, it will serve as a motivating factor to keep them engaged and making the best out of their career.

Collaborators

Growing up, Millennials have been part of an education system that prioritized group work and projects. On top of individual performance, one's group contributions were also a key point of assessment. As a result, Millennials tend to lean into collaboration. This is seen in their preferences to have open workspaces that allow for them to meet other individuals from the same organization. Collaborating with different people on different projects allows for innovation and they enjoy the process of creating new products and processes to add value to their organization. Unlike the Gen Xers, who are commonly known as the latch-key kids because they independently managed their lives since their schooldays, Millennials are much more comfortable working in groups. Gen Xers spent a lot of their childhood independently as they came back to an empty home from school due to both parents being at work. They did their own homework, entertained themselves with the television, and managed their lives independently. Group work was not as common back then and definitely not a part of the school curriculum. Millennials, however, had the privilege of working together with their classmates in groups for various projects that required them to collaborate often. As a result, they have the tendencies to work together in teams.

What This Means for You

As a leader of intergenerational teams, it is important to understand the comfort levels of individuals from different generations. While Millennials may prefer team work, Gen Xers might prefer to work alone in silos. Identifying the strengths of your team members will make it easier for them to work together. Offering opportunities for all to work together on projects will entice this generation. Bringing about a feel of project work from their university days will serve to bring out the best in this group. At the same time, it will give all members of the different generations a better chance of interacting with one another. They will get the opportunities to bond better and learn the working styles and preferences. It will also provide them the chance to develop key soft skills such as running team meetings, giving powerful presentations and learning how to communicate effectively with one another. Use this as an opportunity to bring your team together and build a strong sense of belonging amongst one another.

Like every other generation, the Millennial generation has its unique set of traits and characteristics that were shaped by the financial, social and technological trends during their developmental years. Thanks to globalization, they are much more homogenous than other generations who didn't have access to what was happening around the world. Thanks to the internet, this generation grew up in a closely knit world where they were exposed to the same kind of musicians, entertainment, social media platforms, and the like. Understanding why they are the way they are gives each leader a better sense of what strengths this generation has and how they can better contribute to the teams. In the next chapter, we will dive deep into the first skill that all leaders need to focus on as they start to lead their team members.

Think about it

- What are some of the unique characteristics mentioned above that you relate with?
- What are some of the unique characteristics mentioned above that you do not relate with?
- What are some of the strengths of your generation that you can leverage within your team?
- What are some of the blind spots and weaknesses you notice within your generation that you can cover up with the help of members of different generations?
- What key mindsets, skills, strengths, talents, and competencies do you need for your team to become high performance?
- How can generational diversity add more value to your team?

Chapter 5: Clarity: Leading Yourself before You Lead Others

'We cannot change what we are not aware of, and once we are aware, we cannot help but change.'

—Sheryl Sandberg

It was 'bring your family to work' day at CISCO. The ex-CEO of CISCO John Chambers was giving a speech to close to 500 people full of employees and family members. At one point during his speech, John Chambers noticed that someone had put her hand up, wanting to ask a question. However, it seemed to him that even though she wanted to ask a question, it was obvious and visible that she was really struggling to ask it. Noticing this, John Chambers went closer to the girl and encouraged her to ask the question. Out of nowhere, the girl started to cry, and told him that she had dyslexia. Upon hearing that, John Chambers shared with her that even he himself had dyslexia and even with this condition, he is able to give a speech to a thousand people in the audience which could have presidents and prime ministers, and really senior people, and he would be fine. However, the moment he enters a conversation about dyslexia, his palms begin to sweat as he is taken back to his classroom in West Virginia where kids made fun of him because of his condition.

In an interview with Carmine Gallo, John Chambers shared this incident; he mentioned that he had no idea that he had forgotten to switch off his lapel microphone! As it dawned on him that all those 500 people in the audience heard that he had dyslexia, he panicked. For the longest time, he had always seen being dyslexic as one of his biggest weaknesses. Yet, that evening, after his speech, he had so many messages, emails, and letters where people said 'Thank you for sharing your story. We felt more connected with you today than we ever have.'

John Chambers would have never guessed that showcasing his vulnerability would have inspired others, especially when he thought of it as a weakness. However, the moment John Chambers became aware of how other people related to it positively, it changed the way he looked at dyslexia and inspired him to dive deeper into looking at awareness, not just from his point of view, but from other perspectives as well. That's how powerful clarity can be. When you hit that moment of realization, it serves to provide a stronger perspective to you as a leader.

'The whole problem with the world is that fools and fanatics are always so certain of themselves, and wiser people so full of doubts.'
—Bertrand Russel

Today's organizations are in desperate need of fresh perspectives. Leading is complex enough, but without perspective, it can be overwhelming. As a leader, you need to have a predisposition to perceive and reason in certain ways. You have to be able to simplify the environment and bring a pre-established frame of reference for better understanding. As a leader, not only do you have the potential to impact the people you lead in both positive and negative ways, you also influence their family members and friends indirectly. Developing a perspective as a leader can take time and lots of reflections.

According to Cornell's School of Industrial and Labor Relations that studied seventy-two senior executives at companies with revenues between $50 million and $5 billion, they found that it is not the 'tough guys' who made it to the top. Instead, leaders with high self-awareness formed the basis of strong perspective and interpersonal skills that actually delivered better financial results.

Howard Schultz, Chairman Emeritus of Starbucks, had the perspective that part-time employees should enjoy health benefits. His perspective was formed when he was eleven years old. He tells the story of sitting at a family dinner when his father announced that he had lost his job. Almost immediately, his mother announced that she was pregnant. And they were without insurance. That day, he committed to himself that if he were ever in a position to help others avoid such situations, he would do something about it. Having such a strong perspective comes from having clarity and a high level of self-awareness.

Here's a quick challenge for you.

Try describing yourself to another person without mentioning anything about the external things in your life like your family, friends, where you live or what you do. Concentrate only on yourself, how you feel, what your values are and what keeps you going in life.

Did you struggle with the answer? Looking within for answers is much harder than looking for answers externally. Don't be worried if you did, most people tend to go through life without much perspective. Self-awareness is one of the most important leadership traits you can develop within yourself for life. Although most people believe that they are self-aware, that they know a lot about themselves, true self-awareness is a rare quality. For the last five decades, researchers have used varying definitions for self-awareness. Some see it as the ability to monitor our inner world, whereas others label it as a temporary state of self-consciousness. It is also seen as the difference between how we perceive ourselves and how others perceive us. According to Tasha Eurich, an organizational psychologist and *New York Times* bestselling author of *Insight*, self-awareness is, at its core, the ability to see ourselves clearly to understand who we are, how others see us, and how we fit into the world around us.

The reason we don't develop strong perspectives is because it is harder to do so. Majority of our thoughts and actions are on autopilot. Our habits, routines, impulses, and reactions carry us through our lives so we don't have to stop and think about it every time, for instance like starting a car and heading back home. An autopilot is a system used to control the path of an aircraft, marine craft, or spacecraft without requiring constant manual control by a human operator. Autopilots do not replace human operators; they assist the operator's control of the vehicle, allowing the operator to focus on broader aspects of operations. We as humans are known to have an autopilot function as well.

'Life is not a journey you want to make on autopilot.'

—Paula Rinehart

Have you ever had the experience of driving yourself home without really paying any attention? Brain scans have proven that when your mind wanders, it switches to 'autopilot' mode. This empowers you to carry on doing tasks quickly, accurately, and without conscious thought. According to scientists, the brain has a structure called the 'default mode network' (DMN), that was discovered in the 1990s. In a science experiment, researchers asked twenty-eight volunteers to learn a card game while lying in an fMRI brain scanner. In the game, each person was handed four cards. They were then given a fifth, and asked to match it to one of the four. However, the volunteers were not informed of the rules, hence they didn't know if they were to match the cards by colour or shape. However, with trial and error, each person figured out the pattern after a few rounds. During the experiment, their brain activity resembled patterns that are typical of learning minds. As the game continued, and once participants knew how to match the cards without much thinking, their brain activity portrayed those of using the DMN and their responses became faster and more accurate. People with DMN structures strongly connected, also performed better in the game. This suggests that the more strongly a person's DMN structure is connected, the more effective is their autopilot mode. This is how we as humans tend to 'switch off' and transition into autopilot mode that allows us to perform tasks reasonably without thinking much about them.

The problem is when we are on autopilot, we tend to forget we are in that mode. Sometimes, I have found myself reaching home before I know it and then once I finish parking, I tend to remember that I was supposed to take a detour to buy food for my cat before reaching home. In the end, I find myself starting the car again and heading back to the supermarket. This is where the problem starts, when we forget we are on autopilot. When we are not even aware of our own habits, routines, impulses, and reactions, then we no longer control them— they control us.[30]

Every living system maintains its inner balance, harmony, and order through its capacity to adapt and evolve through the feedback it receives. In nature, there is a constant feedback loop between organisms and their environment for the former to maintain stability. As new circumstances arise, the need to self-regulate increases as well. This is an ever-changing Darwinian dynamic which states that the better the feedback you can get, the better you can regulate yourself and increase your chances of survival. Having an awareness of how we are being perceived from the outside helps us become more aware of what to start, stop, and continue.

According to neuroscientist V.S. Ramachandran, about 150,000 years ago, the human brain developed exponentially. We gained the ability to examine our own thoughts, feelings, and behaviours, as well as to see things from others' point of view. This ability formed the survival advantage for our ancestors who had to work together to stay alive. The ability to evaluate their own behaviours and decisions, and read their impact on other members of the tribe helped them. The advantages of having a high level of self-awareness have not gone away. In the modern world, especially in a post-pandemic one, having high levels of self-awareness allows leaders to make smarter decisions, have better personal and professional relationships, be more creative, and communicate effectively with confidence. The higher you ascend on the corporate ladder, the more important self-awareness becomes. Senior executives who lack self-awareness are 600 per cent more likely to derail and cost companies a staggering $50 million per executive.[31]

---

[30] Manson, Mark. 'The Three Levels of Self-awareness'. *Mark Mansion: Life Advice That Doesn't Stuck.* https://markmanson.net/self-awareness

[31] Eurich, T. 2018. *Insight: The Surprising Truth About How Others See Us, How We See Ourselves, and Why the Answers Matter More Than We Think* (Reprint ed.). Currency.

In her book *Insight*, Tasha Eurich mentions that the biggest misconception of self-awareness is thinking that it's all about looking inwards. Looking inwards will only give you perspective from your own standpoint. You will only be armed with your own observations. Insight from yourself is enlightening, but it is not enough to be fully self-aware. To be truly self-aware, not only do we need to understand how we perceive ourselves, but also how others perceive us. It is entirely possible for us to get valuable insights from other people who are reliable sources of information on how we come across. Self-awareness isn't one truth; it is a complex interweaving of information from two distinct and sometimes even competing viewpoints. Having one without the other will do more harm than good. So the question that remains is: how do we gain more clarity about ourselves?

A thousand prayers can lead to nothing; realization is instant.
—Dr Kesavan Sathyamoorthy, Group CEO,
Diamond Glass Enterprise

Think about a time you booked your car for servicing. Nothing was wrong or broken - the car just needed a mileage check-up. But when you got it back, it drove like a dream. The technicians had made adjustments to parts you never even knew about, and it had made a real difference. Similarly, increasing your self-awareness can help you perform better. Once you know how you operate - what makes you tick - you'll have a good idea of what you can change or adjust to feel better or get better results. You'll find out how you approach life, how you interact with other people and the world, and you'll understand other people's approaches too. Self-awareness is what helps you understand others and how they see you, your temperament, and the way you respond to them in real-time. When leaders see themselves clearly, they make better decisions, build more meaningful relationships, and lead others more effectively. Most first-time leaders are taken aback when they get the results back from a 360-degree feedback in their first year as a leader. Clarity comes to us when we get that jolt from life experiences that really reveals who we really are.

One of my clients related his experience when he returned home on a regular day.

My son and helper were playing. I asked him, where's your mom? They waved to my study room. I went into the room and saw my wife in a frenzy, speaking to her manager. She was laying out her soul, telling her boss exactly how she felt working under her leadership. 'You expected me to work even when I contracted Covid! Not a single word of appreciation from you even when I worked through my sickness. When I had joined, I wasn't given a proper handover and when the new staff just joined, you didn't even bother introducing them to me. It's almost as if I don't even exist! That's it, I'm tendering my resignation today.'

Jolted by the experience, the boss as mentioned above broke down into tears after that conversation and took two days off work because of the shock she got from my client's wife. Awareness doesn't always come from within us, it can be observed from events outside as well.

Back in the army, when we joined as recruits, our sergeant used to shout, 'Wake up your idea' to get us to buck up, change our behaviour and think differently about how things worked around in the army camp. The essence of the phrase basically was to change the way we looked at how we approached life. This phrase is so common amongst those who completed national service in Singapore that it has become a colloquial phrase and is used in conversations. Here are some common situations where one gets to 'wake up their idea' and gain more self-awareness about themselves.

Outside Your Comfort Zone

When we are tasked to do a new role at work or in life, it stretches us from our comfort zone. Have you noticed the roller coaster of emotions you experience when you go through a transition; whether it is from college to a new job, or from being an employee to an entrepreneur, or even from being single to getting into a relationship? All of these new roles you take up reveal more about yourself and can boost your self-awareness. This can come in the form of self-realization or when others share their feedback with you about yourself. I remember the time when I was awarded my first big project that involved managing twenty-four associate trainers for our project. The type of workload that I had really stretched me and revealed how I manage responsibilities as a leader. During that event, one of my trainers came up to me and said, 'Hey, don't try to do everything yourself. You can delegate some of the work to us, we can help you out and things will move faster. If you try to do everything yourself, you will only end up being the bottleneck.' I realized from her sharing that I was not comfortable delegating any responsibilities to others because I was not sure if they would be willing to do the work. Luckily, my trainers came up to me and offered help and I had a realization that day that it was okay for me to delegate responsibilities and divide the workload amongst everyone so that we could get the work done much faster.

An Unexpected Turn of Unfortunate Events

Another situation that raises our levels of self-awareness comes from catastrophes. Typically, events shake us down to the core, because of its severity and significance. Examples of this could be a relationship break up, death or critical illness of a loved one, or a serious setback. When such events are perceived to be life-shattering, it forces us to confront the truth about ourselves. I know of a friend who decided to stop putting up with abuse from her husband after one year of marriage, and decided to leave him for good to protect herself. Coming from an Asian background, worrying about what others would think was a deep concern but she did it anyway. It was a crushing experience for her, yet she had no choice but to stick to this path in order to move on and it led her down a path to better understand how she was behaving and how she usually responds to crises in her life. Such events also tend to paralyze us and suppress our emotional agility. We tend to become more defensive, cynical or shut down completely. The way to avoid this from happening is to absorb the suffering rather than react to it. When my friend decided to leave her husband, she chose to be open to all the feelings that came to her. She chose to understand and be patient with herself and not make harsh decisions. She also committed to empowering herself by taking action based on the new levels of awareness she had about herself.

Eureka Moments

Lastly, self-awareness levels can go up when we have 'Eureka!' moments. The mind has the ability to work on a problem subconsciously. If you've ever had the experience of finding a solution while you were in the shower or doing something noncommittal, such as the house chores, that is what we refer to as a 'Eureka!' moment. When something has been bugging your mind for a while, and when you don't have a solution, it doesn't just disappear. The subconscious mind continues to work on it on some level and when a solution is found, it floats back into our conscious mind and we get an idea that we can try out to solve the problem. Sometimes, a Eureka moment could be a simple random remark that you can question and verify; if the observation holds true for you in most situations. I remember a time when my business partner said, 'How come you're having such a bad running nose? Didn't you sleep well last night?' That comment caught me by surprise, because I had never put those two together. So I asked him how he came to that conclusion. He replied, 'Every time we have camps and you are low on sleep time, you have a bad running nose and flu that lasts the entire day. I've noticed this a few times with you. And it usually disappears once you get enough sleep.' I had never noticed this about myself, but upon introspection, I've come to realize that this is how my body reacts when I don't get enough sleep for a number of days in a row. What was more interesting was that my business partner noticed this about me more than I had. This incident reminded me that even though we may think we know ourselves well, other people who observe us may notice things that are in our blind spot and their revelation only serves to add to our self-awareness. To fully understand the nuances of self-awareness, let me introduce you to the Johari window.

The Four Levels of Self-awareness (Johari Window)

The Johari window is a technique designed to help people better understand their relationship with themselves and others. It was created by psychologists Joseph Luft and Harrinton Ingham. The name of this technique, 'Johari' is a combination of their names.

Imagine a house with four rooms. Room one, Arena, is the part of ourselves that we and others are aware of. Room two, the Blind Spot, is the part of ourselves that others see but we are unaware of. Room three, the Façade, is the private space we know but hide from others. This is what we refer to as the place where we keep our skeletons. Room four, the Unknown, is the unconscious part of us that neither we or others are aware of.

Here is an exercise you can do to find out how you are perceived by yourself and how it compares with how others perceive you.

Step 1:

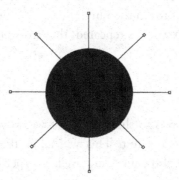

Gather your team or a few closed ones who you feel know you really well. Hand them a piece of paper with the following image on it. Give them one minute to do the exercise. Set a timer that will ring once time is up. All they need to do within this one minute, is to write the name of the person (in this case, you) in the center of the circle and write down all the adjectives that they can use to describe or associate with you. You don't have to over-explain any of the instructions, it is as simple as this. Then, once you start the timer, you also have to write eight words that you would use to describe yourself. No one is allowed to talk or look at each others' answers because you want everyone to write what comes to their minds quickly. Overthinking can reduce the accuracy of the exercise.

Step 2:

Once the timer rings, everyone puts their pens down. Then, one by one, everyone shares the eight words that they have written about you. Here is where it gets interesting. If someone writes Charismatic and others also write the same word, that word goes into the 'Arena' box under Johari's Window, which indicates that everyone is aware of this characteristic of the person.

Those words that others have a general consensus of, but do not match the eight words you wrote to describe yourself, and seems like new information to you, goes into room two, the 'Blind Spot'. Usually, when people share their eight words, some of those words will be synonyms that mean the same thing, and they will keep getting repeated. The more a word is repeated, the stronger association people have of that word with you.

Step 3:

The last and final step is to share the eight words you have selected to describe yourself with the rest. This will allow them to see how you perceive yourself and also gauge how well they perceive you. This step helps your team or your loved ones understand how well they know you. After this, to have a deeper analysis of the words that you have gathered from the rest, you can get the team members to explain why they picked the words they did from the 'Blind Spot'. Their explanations of the words, with examples of how they came to associate you with that particular word, will reveal how they are perceiving you and give you a greater sense of clarity and heightened self-awareness. After everyone is done sharing their perspectives, you too can share your thoughts on what you learned. Here are some questions to think about:

Think about it

- How easy or difficult was it to come up with adjectives to describe yourself? Why?
- How easy or difficult was it for others to come up with adjectives to describe you? Why?
- What were some of the expected words, and what were some of the unexpected words?
- Why were they unexpected?
- What did you get to learn more about yourself from doing this exercise?
- What can you do to reduce your Blind Spot and move those traits into your Arena instead?
- How can you apply what you learned about you and your teammates to improve collaboration?

Try it out with a few people whom you believe know you well to a certain extent, and you will be amazed with the results. This exercise has always brought about lots of laughter as well as highlighted many of the deeper insights into how one is perceived and remembered. As for the Façade and the Unknown, we won't need to put words into those rooms because the Façade is your room of secrets and what is unknown to others and unknown to yourself, is irrelevant to you as well. From this Johari window exercise, you get to distinguish what you already know about yourself—which is in your conscious mind—with what you don't know about yourself. Sometimes this can be because you haven't gotten the feedback from others, or sometimes it could also be because you haven't really spent enough time with yourself to explore some important questions that define who you are. In order to do that, here's a Japanese concept and exercise that can help you discover more about yourself.

Identify Your Ikigai

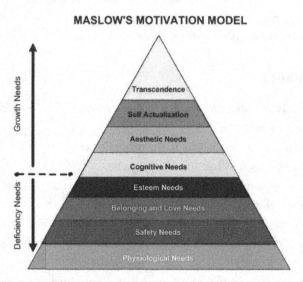

[Source: https://commons.wikimedia.org/wiki/File:Maslow%27s_
Hierarchy_of_Needs.webp.png]

The human race is always evolving, not just physically, but in terms of thought as well. Over the decades, we have seen maturity in terms of thinking with every passing generation. According to Maslow's hierarchy of needs, there are different stages of needs for the human being. Currently, we are living in the most comfortable of times compared to the past. As our deficiency needs (as shown in figure 1.1 above) have been taken care of, we move towards growth needs where we seek meaning. We see this trend happening as Millennials are much more interested in working in meaningful jobs that have a direct impact in making the world a better place. According to Horizon Media, 81 per cent of Millennials expect companies to publicly pledge to be good corporate citizens.[32] One of the top buzzwords that have come up in

---

[32] Rudominer, Ryan. 5 February 2016. 'Corporate Social Responsibility Matters: Ignore Millennials at Your Peril'. *Huffpost*. https://www.huffpost.com/entry/corporate-social-

one's dictionary, which didn't exist for the previous generations, is Ikigai. You've probably heard the word, or seen this four-circle diagram below before.

The term ikigai is composed of *iki* and *gai*. *Iki* refers to 'life'; *gai* means the 'realization of what one expects and hopes for'. To put it simply, Ikigai means to have a reason for being, the reason for which you wake up in the morning, and your reason to live.

Here are the four areas to look into to identify your Ikigai.

[Source:https://commons.wikimedia.org/wiki/File:Ikigai-ES-TrWikiCommons.png]

What You Love

This sphere includes what you do that brings you the most joy in life and makes you feel most alive and fulfilled. What you might love in this sense may be sailing, writing poetry, rock climbing, cooking, traveling, or reading books. What is important is that you allow yourself to think deeply about all the things you love. A quick way to identify activities that you really enjoy doing is when you go into a state of flow. According to psychologist Mihály Csíkszentmihályi in 1975, a flow state is the mental state when a person is performing some activity by being fully immersed in a feeling of energized focus, full involvement and enjoyment in the process of the activity. In essence, flow is characterized by the complete absorption in what one does, and a resulting transformation in one's sense of time. When you experience flow, you will not notice how time passes by. A common misconception that people have is that there is only one item that fits into each circle. That is not true. In a world where we are shifting towards a gig economy, having multiple passions is a strength that you can possibly monetize in the future. Making time for those hobbies that you enjoyed doing but left because you got busy or thought you couldn't leverage might come in handy in the future.

Think about it

- If all professions paid you the same salary, would you still be doing the same job you are doing right now?
- List out all the different things you are passionate about without focusing on the money aspect.
- Has there been any particular activity that you have been so involved in that you lost track of time?

What You are Good At

This sphere includes anything you are particularly good at, such as skills that you have learnt, hobbies that you have pursued, or talents that you have showcased since a young age, etc. What you are good at might be simple things such as being a good listener, public speaker, coder, negotiator, or painter. The way you identify what you are good at is to see what has come easily to you. Writing comes easily for me, and over time, I realized that it was something that others actually struggled with. Similarly, I have struggled with video editing, whereas my video editor friend loves the process of editing raw footage and making it much better than what it was when shot. Knowing what you are talented at is crucial because great management typically comes from playing to your strengths as opposed to fixating your weaknesses.

Another way to identify what you are good at is to think back to all the unsolicited compliments you have received from others. Do they compliment your writing, your skills in art, your ability to get the best deals online, your ability to hold the attention of a group while speaking in public, your ability to make others laugh? Go back to the previous exercise on the Johari window and check your notes from that exercise. Do you remember the common compliments that you have received consistently over time? Even if you may not have considered those as compliments seriously because it came from someone close, or because it is something that comes easily to you, do not discard it entirely. Lean in to those comments that people make about you and really reflect on it. If others are picking up on your strengths, it clearly means you are onto something that makes you stand out.

Being in Asia, we are known to deflect all positive compliments because we are taught to be 'humble'. This is a huge misconception people have. Downplaying yourself and your accomplishments is not humility, it's modesty. Modesty means relatively low or small in amount. According to Brené Brown, author of *Atlas of the Heart*, humility just means openness to new learnings and at the same time having a very balanced assessment of your own contributions. It means putting out what you need to put out about yourself but at the same time willing to listen to others. Adam Grant, another prolific author, mentions in *Think Again*, that 'Intellectual humility is when you share a point of view, have a point of view, but you're also open to what others have to say. Deciding not to accept compliments or asserting your strengths as a leader is not humility. It's modesty. It's time we get this right. Knowing your strengths is not the same as bragging about it. So keep your ears open for any positive comments that may come from your inner circle or from your colleagues'.

Think about it

- What comes easily to you that others have found hard to do themselves?
- What are some unsolicited compliments you have received in the last three months?
- What are the top three most common pieces of positive feedback that you've received from your leaders or colleagues?

What You can be Paid for

This dimension of the diagram refers to the world or society at large, where it involves what someone else might be willing to pay you for or 'what the market will bear'. You might be passionate about writing poetry or very good at dancing, but this does not necessarily mean that you will be compensated for it. As much as passion and strengths are important, one must also carefully consider if the offerings that they have for the world is something that is in demand. If no one sees the demand for your painting or your poetry, it will be hard to make a living out of it. This is why it is important to understand the market really well. Are there role models in your country or state, doing things that you would like to be doing? With social media becoming the norm for most of us to stay connected, even skills like setting up a profile on LinkedIn or writing posts that garner attention or grow your followers can be something you can get paid for outside of your day job. I know of video editors who work full time and take up extra gigs on the side because there is a market for them. People who can drive vehicles can earn a living today because there is a demand for delivery services in the logistics sector. As Anthony Robbins always says, 'Success leaves clues', and all you need to do is identify others who are doing what you would like to be doing and model them.

Unfortunately, a lot of passions have been squashed by parents because they have not seen certain professions thrive in society. When people struggle to make ends meet, their needs drop to the basic ones as Maslow indicates, where one is looking purely for physiological, safety, belonging and esteem-based needs. However, times have changed so much since then. Today, the very people who told you to 'find a real job' are the ones struggling to stay relevant and hold on to their existing jobs as they are replaced with artificial intelligence and technology. The roles of the future are yet to be defined, and much of the mechanical work that can be done by robots will snatch away jobs of those who have been comfortable doing the routine work. As technology gets smarter, more of the boring and routine work will be done by devices instead of people. Therefore, it always pays to stay relevant by staying agile and having a pulse of what is in demand in the marketplace.

Think about it

- What are some skills you have that you believe you can get paid outside of your current job for?
- What other alternate careers could you pursue with the skills you have gathered till now?
- What other alternate careers could you pursue by acquiring new certifications and skills by upgrading yourself?

What the World Needs

If you have a business idea that solves a problem that people face multiple times a day, you have a billion-dollar business.

—Jeff Bezos

For instance, Google. People have lots of questions on a daily basis and Google has the answers. Similarly, in the corporate world, the change we want to make is about the things that happen all the time. Sometimes we have the digital tool but there is no adoption. Other times the management wants diversity, equity and inclusion but people don't know how to implement it. These high frequency stories, things that happen all the time, are where we can look to for clues, and they will help you tremendously to heighten your level of awareness of the issues that we face on a conscious level.

The final dimension of the diagram refers to the needs of the planet that is sustaining us. The 'world' here might be humanity as a whole, a small community you are in touch with, or anything in between. What the world needs might be based on your impressions or needs expressed by others. The world's needs might include skilled nursing, clean water, ending poverty and many other things. This is why the United Nations came up with the 2030 agenda for sustainable development that provides a shared blueprint for peace and prosperity for the people and the planet, now and into the future. At its heart are the seventeen Sustainable Development Goals (SDGs) which are an urgent call for action by all countries in a global partnership. Aligning yourself to a goal will contribute to the SDGs and help you see the impact you make in making the world a better place.

Think about it

- Which of the seventeen SDGs appeal the most to you? Why?
- What can you do in your own small way to contribute to the seventeen SDGs?
- Can you pick one of the SDGs for your personal contribution and one that fits in well under your company's contribution?

Ikigai Happens when it all Comes Together

When you get to align all four circles together, one experiences Ikigai. The sweet spot within this Ikigai diagram would therefore involve something you are passionate about, that you are also good at, that the world needs now, and for which someone will pay you. Identifying one's Ikigai has not been so much of a priority for the older generations as it has been with the younger ones. Given the better circumstances that they have lived in, the needs that appeal to the younger generation often falls in the higher needs based on Maslow's motivation model. Similarly, the older generations' needs are much more focused on the deficiency needs because they value that. Either way, as a leader, you will have to have clarity over what your Ikigai looks like so that you can learn how to guide your team members to identify the same for themselves. The reason for doing this is purely to have a better understanding of what your drivers are in life. Understanding your passion gives you guidance on what to pursue, knowing your strengths gives you the confidence of what you are capable of, finding out what the world can pay you to ensure that it is practical enough for you to pursue it and doing something for the world in general gives you a bigger-than-life purpose. Overall, it gives you a sense of satisfaction and a reason for being. Now that we have worked on understanding the big picture, we will start to dive deeper into the nuances of who you are. This includes finding out more about the patterns you display—consciously or subconsciously—as well as biases you may hold that affects how you appear as a leader at work.

Understanding Your Patterns

Human beings enjoy categorizing things. It facilitates our understanding of relationships between things or concepts that might seem otherwise unrelated, as well as creates initial connections that in turn build relationships. People who are high in self-awareness tend to make decisions that are in congruence with themselves, allowing them to lead happier and more satisfying lives. Those without it act in ways that are incompatible with their true success and happiness, like staying in a job where abuse is the norm and not the exception. Having an understanding of your behaviour from the outside-in is also a key part of self-awareness. Those leaders who have their pulse on the ground about how they are being perceived are able to build stronger and more trusting relationships. Now, while not all of us may have the time or ability to know how others perceive us, there are tools that actually show us what patterns we tend to display, based upon a large number of people researched. That is why we see an array of personality profiling tools that have grouped different traits and behaviours together. It is not an uncommon observance to see individuals perform much better once they get a better insight into who they are and why they are the way they are through the help of a personality profiling tool and a profiling coach.

We have preferences for all sorts of things; for instance, most of us prefer to use one hand rather than the other for writing. Having a preference doesn't mean that you can't do things in a different way; if you are left-handed, you can probably write with your right hand if you need to. In the same way, we all have preferences when it comes to our personality. Preferences do not indicate skill or ability. If your preferred hand were injured, you would still be able to use your non-preferred hand but doing so may take more effort. Types are made of preferences and there are no 'right' or 'wrong' types. Each has its strengths and blind spots.

Personality profiling isn't about identifying the ideal; it is not about what is right or wrong. Every personality type has its pros and cons, learning what situations you work best in and how you like to do things, and understanding the same for your colleagues so that everyone can feel comfortable and supported to give their best in their role.

Personality Profiling Doesn't Box You in, It Sets You Free

The intention behind personality profiling tools is not to stereotype or 'put people in a box', but rather to help them understand themselves and others in a simple, easy-to-remember way. When you understand your personality profile fully, it frees you in several ways. It gives you confidence in your own direction of development: the areas in which you can become excellent with the most ease and pleasure. It can also reduce the guilt many people feel at not being able to do everything in life equally well. For most people, really understanding their own type in particular and other people's types in general, is a releasing experience rather than a restricting one. It sets one free to recognize one's own natural bent and to trust one's own potential for growth and excellence with no obligation to copy anyone else, however admirable that person may be in his or her own different way. Acknowledging your own preferences opens up the possibility of finding constructive values instead of conflicts in the differences you encounter with someone whose preferences are opposite to yours.

People are inherently complex. It often takes a lot of time to get to really know someone and understand how that person does things and why they do them. However, there are patterns in how people behave and their motivations. With time, as we get to know our friends and colleagues better, we often build up an idea of how we are similar and how we differ. Personality profiling tools are simply another way of building up that picture and understanding others better. Every person is a unique individual but we all share certain characteristics. Your personality profile shows your preferences that are common with others who share the same personality profile. They also highlight how you might be different from others with a different personality from yours. Personality profiling is one tool that you can use to gain insight into the common patterns of your behaviour such as understanding how you prefer to learn, work and interact. Using this information you can then focus on creating a work environment that is conducive to productivity for your team.

The Myers-Briggs test has gained popularity as a deeply insightful and accurate profile of characteristics within a person. It was created by Isabel Briggs Myers and her mother Katherine. The test is based on Carl Jung's psychological types that categorizes individuals into one of sixteen types. These types are four letter acronyms divided on four dichotomies that indicate the different ways a person perceives and relates to the world and others around them.

This tool focuses on telling you how your brain prefers to organize and absorb the world, how it tends to form opinions, beliefs, and make decisions based on that absorbed information, and most importantly, how open or closed your brain is to changing when new information is provided. The essence of the theory is that much of the seemingly random variation in the behaviour is actually quite orderly and consistent, being due to basic differences in the ways individuals prefer to use their perception and judgment. It is used to measure psychological preferences in how people perceive the world and make decisions.

Note that the terms used for each dichotomy have specific technical meanings relating to the MBTI which differ from their everyday usage. For instance, people who prefer judgment over perception are not necessarily more judgmental or less perceptive. The MBTI instrument sorts for preference and does not measure trait, ability, or character. No instrument can do that. This assessment wasn't designed to predict who will be most successful in certain occupations, and there's no evidence to indicate that certain MBTI types are more successful in certain careers. What it can do is identify which MBTI types are attracted to and over represented in certain occupations. In fact, examining this attraction and over-representation is one of the primary methods of validating the MBTI assessment. For instance, when an over-representation of ISTJs is found in accounting jobs, it suggests that certain types are attracted to certain careers. However, when interpreting this kind of occupational data, two factors are important to remember.

First, data showing attraction to an occupation should not be interpreted as being indicative of high performance in that occupation. Second, while the research shows that certain types are over-represented in certain occupations, it also shows that all 16 types are represented in almost every occupation. Simply put, certain types are known to flock towards certain professions, and at the same time, it does not indicate that they are any better in terms of trait, ability or character for that profession. So for instance, it is a tool that can explore patterns (by looking at data) but it cannot be used to chart careers (looking forward) although it can showcase what the patterns have been so far and based on those patterns, suggestions can be made.

That doesn't mean that if I look at the data, and a personality consultant suggests, I try, for instance, engineering as a career (because it happens to be where most INTPs seem to end up in terms of career options). The MBTI type doesn't, in any way, suggest that I have 1) the ability, 2) the character, or 3) the traits to be successful in it. It merely suggests that people who have my type, in large part, have gone on to take up engineering as a career option. That doesn't mean I will not succeed in a career as a scientist or a lawyer just because INTPs are not over represented in such careers.[33]

It simply indicates one preference over another. Someone reporting a high score for extraversion over introversion cannot be correctly described as more extraverted: they simply have a clear preference to being extraverted. Point scores on each of the dichotomies can vary considerably from person to person, even amongst those with the same type. According to Isabel Myers, the direction of the preference (i.e. E vs I) is more important than the degree of the preference (i.e. extreme preference vs slight preference). The expression of a person's psychological type is more than the sum of the four individual preferences.

Jung's typological model regards psychological type as similar to left or right handedness. Some prefer to be right-handed, some prefer to be left-handed. Similarly, some are either born with, or

---

[33] 2 October 2018. 'MBTI Facts & Common Criticisms'. *The Myers-Briggs Company*. https://www.themyersbriggs.com/en-US/Connect-with-us/Blog/2018/October/MB-TI-Facts--Common-Criticisms

develop, certain preferred ways of thinking and acting. The MBTI sorts some of these psychological differences into four opposite pairs, or dichotomies, resulting in sixteen possible psychological types. None of these types are better or worse; however, Briggs and Myers theorized that individuals naturally prefer one overall combination over the other types. Just like how writing with the left hand is hard work for a right-hander, some people tend to find using their opposite psychological preferences more difficult, even if they can become more proficient with practice and development.

The sixteen types are typically referred to by an abbreviation of four letters—the initial letters of each of their four type preferences. For instance
- ESTP: Extraversion (E), Sensing (S), Thinking (T), Perception (P)
- INTJ: Introversion (I), Intuition (N), Feeling (F), Judgment (J)

Four dichotomies:

Extraversion (E)–(I) Introversion
Sensing (S)–(N) Intuition
Thinking (T)–(F) Feeling
Judgment (J)–(P) Perception

How You Get Your Energy: Introvert vs Extrovert

The extraversion–introversion dichotomy was first explored by psychologist Carl Jung in this theory of personality types as a way to describe how people respond and interact with the world around them. Extraverts are 'outward-turning' and tend to be action-oriented, enjoy frequent social interactions, and feel energized after spending time with other people. People who prefer extraversion draw energy from action; they tend to act, reflect on their actions, and then act further. If they are inactive, their motivation tends to decline. To rebuild their energy, extraverts need breaks from time spent in reflection. Conversely, those who prefer introversion expend energy through action. Introverts are 'inward-turning' and tend to be thought-oriented, enjoy deep and meaningful social interactions, and feel recharged after spending time alone, away from activity. A common misconception of introverts is that they are reserved or shy but it is actually how they derive energy from their inner world. We all exhibit extraversion and introversion to some degree, but most of us tend to have an overall preference for one or the other. Based on the two possibilities, which one do you find yourself leaning more towards? Circle your preference.

Think about it

- Based on the two possibilities, which one do you find yourself leaning more towards? Circle your preference.
  (I) Introvert / (E) Extrovert

How You Take in Information and Learn: Sensing vs Intuition

Sensing and Intuition are the information-gathering functions. This scale involves looking at how people gather information from the world around them. They describe how new information is understood and interpreted. People who prefer sensing are more likely to trust information that is in the present, tangible, and concrete. In other words, information that can be understood by the five senses. They tend to distrust hunches or gut feeling, which tend to come out of 'nowhere'. They prefer to look at facts and details. For them, the meaning is in the data. People who prefer sensing tend to pay a great deal of attention to reality, particularly to what they can learn from their own senses. They tend to focus on facts and details and enjoy getting hands-on experience.

Those who prefer intuition tend to trust information that is less dependent on the five senses, that can be associated with other information and pay more attention to things like patterns and impressions. They enjoy thinking about possibilities, imagining the future, and abstract theories. They tend to look at the world with 'the whole is greater than the sum of parts' philosophy. For them, meaning is in the underlying theory and principles which are manifested in the data. Similar to the extraversion and introversion dichotomy, all people spend time sensing and intuiting depending on the situation.

According to the MBTI, people tend to be dominant in one area or the other. Based on the two possibilities, which one do you find yourself learning more towards? Circle your preference.

Think about it

- Based on the two possibilities, which one do you find yourself leaning more towards? Circle your preference.
  (S) Sensing / (N) Intuition

How You Make Decisions: Thinking vs Feeling

Thinking and Feeling are decision-making functions. The thinking and feeling functions are both used to make rational decisions, based on the information-gathering functions (sensing or intuition). Those who prefer thinking tend to decide things from a more detached standpoint, measuring the decision by what seems reasonable, logical, causal, consistent, and matching a given set of rules. Those who prefer feeling tend to come to decisions by associating or empathizing with the situation, looking at it 'from the inside' and weighing the situation to achieve, on balance, the greatest harmony, consensus and fit, considering the needs of the people involved.

Thinkers usually have trouble interacting with people who are inconsistent or illogical, and tend to give very direct feedback to others. They are concerned with the truth and view it as more important. As mentioned previously, people who prefer thinking do not necessarily, in the everyday sense, 'think better' than their feeling counterparts, in the common sense and in the same vein, those who prefer feeling do not necessarily have 'better' emotional reactions than their thinking counterparts. Based on the two possibilities, which one do you find yourself learning more towards? Circle your preference.

Think about it

- Based on the two possibilities, which one do you find yourself leaning more towards? Circle your preference.
  (T) Thinking / (F) Feeling

How You Like to Organize Your Time and Environment: Judging vs Perceiving

This scale involves how people tend to deal with the outside world. These two tendencies interact with the other dichotomies. This pair describes whether you act in the outer world when you are making decisions or when you are taking in information. Some people interact with the outside world when they are taking in outside information. Whether they use the sensing preference or intuitive preference, they are still interacting with the outside world. Other people do their interacting when they are making decisions. It doesn't matter if they are using a thinking preference or a feeling preference, they are still interacting with the outside world. Everyone takes in information some of the time. Everyone makes decisions some of the time. However, when it comes to dealing with the outer world, people who tend to focus on making decisions have a preference for judging because they tend to like things decided. People who tend to take in information prefer perceiving because they stay open to a final decision in order to get more information.

Think about it

- Based on the two possibilities, which one do you find yourself leaning more towards? Circle your preference.
  (J) Judging / (P) Perceiving

While it is not possible to get an accurate analysis purely based on the brief descriptions laid out here, this is a simple way of identifying what you are aware of in terms of your personality. Based on your own personal analysis, write down the letters that you have circled in the order you circled it. This is known as your *type*. Type is more than just the sum of the four preferences. The four-letter MBTI type formula is a shorthand way of telling you about the interaction of your four mental functions and which ones you prefer to use first.

This is called type dynamics and it is an important part of understanding your MBTI results. If you would like to have an accurate idea of what your personality is like, you can purchase the personality profiling tool online and get in touch with a certified MBTI practitioner like myself to evaluate what you have guessed with what the system has analyzed based on the answers from the MBTI questionnaire. They both need to go hand-in-hand to get the most accurate results. The image below shows the sixteen possibilities that your personality type might fall under and the typical patterns that can be observed by the different personality types. If you are interested to learn more about your personality and dive deeper into identifying your conscious and subconscious behaviours, feel free to connect with me through LinkedIn at www.linkedin.com/in/millennialexpertasia.

[Source: https://commons.wikimedia.org/wiki/
File:MyersBriggsTypes.png]

Understanding your patterns through your personality is one of the fastest ways you can enhance your clarity about yourself. While it does not have to be limited to any personality profiling tool in particular, it is useful to every leader to have an idea of themselves and the patterns they display at work. I highly recommend you to invest in personality profiling tools in order to lead better.

So far, we have covered bases on how we can raise awareness of the issues that remain in our conscious level. Unfortunately, we have other issues as well that remain buried in our subconscious level that leaders also need to be aware of. These issues consist of unconscious bias and stereotypes that we tend to pick up from our environment and sometimes it remains in the background and overshadows all the actions we take in the workplace. Dr David Rock, the Director of Neuroleadership Institute and co-editor of the *Neuroleadership Journal,* coined the term 'neuroleadership' to explain how the unconscious part of our brain handles change, collaboration and leadership style. Rock's research suggests that the brain craves certainty and avoids uncertainty whenever possible. The brain sees uncertainty as a threat and the threat tends to trigger alert responses in the limbic system. The more ambiguity in any decision-making process, the greater the threat response in the brain. Similarly, the lower the ambiguity level, the greater the sensation of reward. Therefore, the human brain is always on the lookout for ways to create certainty in the world; on conscious or unconscious levels. The way we tend to do this is by categorizing things and labeling things around us. The labels we assign to the people and things around us help alleviate the sense of unpredictability. They allow us to believe that we know enough to understand and possibly predict and prevent any forms of danger.

Rock's neuroleadership theory also demonstrates how the brain tends to convert predictions into convictions. The brain gathers information, converts the information into patterns, stores the patterns as memories, which then become the foundation of beliefs that guide predictions for the future. Predicting patterns is a pleasure trigger that leads us to search for more patterns and predictability. We experience this in simple, everyday situations. When a stranger walks into a room, we instantly form a judgment about him or her based on appearances. We look at the clothes he or she is wearing, the way he or she stands, his hair, skin color, and age is all taken into account and processed within seconds to form a judgment. This judgment is based on the previous information that we might have gathered in the past through our education, upbringing, and experiences which have been converted into memories. Our brain, in its efforts to save energy, will go into prediction mode based on what information we already have about the person.

When this happens, unfortunately, we don't take the time to get to know the person in front of us. Since the pleasure center in our brain is triggered based on our prediction, we do not always revise our first impressions or remain open to the reality that actually exists before us. If you have at any point in time believed in the phrase, 'You never get a second chance to make a first impression', it is because this is how people primarily function across the board.

Mahzarin Banaji, a Harvard professor who actually studies bias, once adamantly refused to talk to a persistent reporter until the reporter told her that she was an alum of Banaji's college.

'I heard that and the words "Come on over, I'll talk to you" suddenly came out of my mouth. All my rational reasons for not talking to her went out of the window because we shared a zip code for four years.'[34]

According to Banaji, research shows that we use different parts of our brain to deal with those who are more similar to us and those who are different. We internalize stereotypes. We judge trustworthiness within microseconds of meeting people based on little more than facial features. As a result, these unconscious biases shape judgments about character, abilities and potential.

The reality is that our attitudes and behaviour towards other people can be influenced as much by our instinctive feelings as by our rational thought processes. And that hidden drive affects everything, from who you hire to who you will pick to run the next meeting. Our brains are hardwired to make unconscious decisions, because the number of choices we face every day would be overwhelming if we had to consciously evaluate every single one. That means there is a direct link between our unconscious thinking and our actions and behaviour. And when it comes to making choices at work, it is important to know they are not based on bias.

How We Stereotype

While we may not be aware of our prejudices, and prefer not to admit them if we are biased, they can have damaging consequences

---

[34] 18 March 2013. 'Take Five: Tips for Uncovering Bias.' *Duke Today.* https://today.duke. edu/2013/03/takefivediversity

on both the way we manage and the people we manage. Studies have shown that perceived discrimination—how people feel when they're being discriminated against—can affect various elements of their performance and the people we manage such as their commitment levels, job satisfaction and work tension. Leaders can be influenced by unconscious bias when conducting performance reviews. If your team members suspect this to be true, it can lead to mistrust, lowered morale and an increased likelihood of good people leaving your organization. It is because of these unconscious biases that we are still struggling to see diversity, equity and inclusion in the workplace. Why is it that women are missing from senior management roles? Why do people of color struggle with getting job promotions? Why do we see the LGBTQI community and others who are different struggling to get employment in the workplace? It is because we are still being driven by these unconscious biases that are deep seated within us. When we start grouping people based on these differences, we give them a label and outcast them. According to social psychologists Henri Tajfel and John Turner, this is what is known as in-group and out-group dynamics to explain social identity. This theory describes the process by which we classify people as 'us' or 'them'. Tajfel and Turner posit that this process takes place in three steps: social categorization, social identification, and social comparison. In the first step, social categorization, we categorize things in order to understand them. Our ability to categorize the world is necessary for us to survive. It helps us to understand the world more simply and helps remove some of the ambiguity with which our brain is uncomfortable. This is the first step that leads to stereotypes.

How Categorization Leads to Identification

The second step is social identification, where once the categories are in place, we identify with the category. For instance, across the globe, we identify ourselves as citizens of different countries. We look into the common behaviours that each citizen of the particular nationality identifies with. Singaporeans are known to identify with the Singaporean English, which is also known as Singlish, which is a mix of English with a bit of Mandarin, Hokkien, Tamil, and Malay.

This is a shared identity. A sense of self understanding and pride comes with being affiliated with a group. Even the Singaporean Chinese here like to identify themselves differently from the China Chinese who are immigrants from China. Even though in terms of physical appearance, both Chinese individuals may look similar, they identify themselves very differently.

Identification Precedes Social Comparison

The final step in the social-identity process is social comparison, the process of comparing our group (the in-group) to the others (the out-group). To build self-esteem, members of the in-group must see themselves as better than the out-group. This is how teams are formed and rivalries are perpetuated. Ask any football fan from Manchester United or Liverpool, they will always see themselves as better than the other group for various reasons. This boosts the loyalty, status and self-esteem of the group members and also serves to deflate the status of the out-group. According to Tajfel and Turner, the characteristics we acquire as a result of identifying with a group are not artificial; they are real characteristics, adopted and practiced so that they become vital to a our identity. However, many are not conscious of their own biases and blind spots. Moreover, biases can only be reduced rather than completely eliminated and it is difficult to control biases that are unconscious. Leaders are under extraordinary pressure right now. They are expected to make decisions quickly with incomplete and rapidly evolving information. And unfortunately, being in crisis mode can cause even the most intentional and well-meaning leaders to fall into patterns of bias and exclusion. Research by Science Direct shows that when we are stressed, we often default to gut instincts rather than making deliberate and goal-oriented decisions.[35]

Now is a time for leaders to think about what type of leader they need to be for all their team members, especially for the most vulnerable and marginalized ones. As we move from rapid response to short term to long term recovery, community, connection, and allyship with a

---

[35] https://www.sciencedirect.com/science/article/pii/S2352289515300187

deep awareness of how implicit bias shows up in decision making will become really important leadership competencies.

Therefore, to gain awareness of your biases, you need to be honest with yourself about the stereotypes that affect you. Say you've got two of your team members in mind for a promotion. Both David and Jean have great skills and it is a difficult decision, but you decide to go with Jean because she seems to have good ideas about marketing your product. You feel like you have made the right choice, based on evidence. But what if the decision was actually based on something else, without you being aware of it? As difficult as it might be to admit, it is possible to be unconsciously biased regarding race, gender, age, social class, and more. Could your decision not to pick David be because of his gender? For example, you may believe consciously that men and women are equally effective leaders but, as a woman, you believe that men perhaps don't have the same level of empathy and people skills as women. That subconscious bias could influence your actions as a leader when you are looking to choose candidates for certain positions or roles. The first step that leaders need to take to reduce bias at the workplace is to ensure they become aware of their own implicit biases.

Neurological tests and exercises can uncover unconscious biases and reduce their influence. One way to reveal your own unconscious bias is by taking the Implicit Association Test (IAT). It is created by researchers from Harvard, Virginia and Washington universities. This test measures the strength of links you make between concepts like race or generations or sexuality, and evaluation of stereotypes, such as whether those concepts are good or bad. Research by R. Turner on 'imagined intergroup contact' has shown that simply visualizing a particular situation can create the same behavioural and psychological effects as actually experiencing it. For example, in tests, participants who imagined a strong woman later showed less gender stereotyping than people who had imagined a vacation.[36]

---

[36] Turner, R, Crisp, R. J., Husnu, S., & Stathi, S. December 2018. 'Imagined Intergroup Contact: Theory, Paradigm, and Practice'. *Academia.edu*. https://www.academia.edu/676316/Imagined_intergroup_contact_Theory_paradigm_and_practice

There are other ways to reduce your bias. Declare your intentions about valuing a diverse workforce. Saying words out loud, or writing them down, sends a clear message to everyone you work with, as well as to your own subconscious. Moreover, exposure to negative stereotypes can reinforce their influence on your behaviour, even if you don't consciously agree with them, so consider providing positive images in the workplace, for example, using posters, newsletters, reports, videos, and podcasts. Surround yourself with positive words and images about people you might have negative stereotypical thoughts about, to help eliminate biases. Gender inequality exists in more places than we can imagine, especially in the most common of places.

Caroline Criado Perez writes in her book *Invisible Women*, about a joke made by a government official that revealed how biased their policies were. Back in 2011, in a town called Karlskoga in Sweden, officials were being hit by the gender inequality conversation and as a result, they had to look through all their policies through the gender lens. As their policies were going through such a harsh glare, one unfortunate official made the comment, 'Well, at least snow clearing is not something these gender people can poke their noses into!'

He said that remark offhandedly, because how can snow clearing have anything to do with gender inequality!

That exact comment got the Gender activists to ask themselves the question, 'Is snow clearing sexist?'

Guess what they found! This process of clearing snow was seen as a process that is favourable to men and not women.

Well, the normal way to clear snow was to first clear these high traffic areas where the cars would drive. Then, they would clear the pedestrian pathways, and then they would proceed to clear the bicycle pathways. At first instance, you would not assume there is anything about gender bias in how snow gets cleared. But here's where it gets even more interesting.

It was discovered that most men drive and a lot of women take public transport or walk. Another thing to note here, is that if there was a household with one car, even in a country that is known to be the utopia of feminism, Sweden, men would take that car and women would actually end up taking public transport or walking to places. Even the travel patterns between men and women were different.

Men usually go to work, come back from work and that's pretty much it. Women however, tend to do what is known as 'trip chaining'. What it essentially means is that they fit in a lot of trips with one trip. So if they're out of their house for the day to drop their children off at school, on their way back, they go pick up groceries and meet up with friends all in one trip. So their travel patterns are a lot more complex. When officials learned about this from the gender people, who supported it with a lot of data points, they decided that they might as well change the pattern. Instead of clearing the roads of snow for cars first, they decided to clear snow from paths of pedestrians and public transport users first. Clearing snow for cars went down the priority list. Moreover, it was much easier to drive through 3-inch snow in comparison to pushing a buggy through the snow to clear the roads for cars.

What the officials didn't realize at that time was that after they made that change was that they would also end up saving a lot of money because with that data, they ended up finding out that a lot of the injuries that were reported to the hospitals around the time when it snowed heavily were from pedestrians, not motorcyclists or drivers. And a lot of those injured were women! So when officials changed their policy to prioritize clearing snow on pedestrian pathways and public transport pathways, the number of injuries also reduced and as a result, they saved a lot of money.

When we adopt the mindset of 'This is one place you will never find gender inequality', we fail to realize that most of our biases exist in places where we assert with confidence that this will never happen. This is where we need to interrogate those areas to spot and break our biggest biases. The biggest bias, as they say, is 'I'm not biased'. So the next time you hear such confident statements like 'This would never happen in our organization' or 'This would never happen here' at the workplace, be brave enough to probe and interrogate further in that exact place to find and break the biases that exist. Larry Page, co-founder of Google said,

To sum it up, everyone has a subconscious bias. They are simply the brain's way of coping with and categorizing all the information we receive every day. Our tendency to discriminate against a group or person may not be intentional, but we can still do something to change it. The more we expose ourselves to ideas, images and words that challenge negative stereotypes, the less discriminatory we will be. We have to raise our awareness of our biases, accept that we do have biases and we are not perfect, and adapt accordingly to become better leaders for the people following our lead.

Two days after the Taliban took over Afghanistan, a woman with red eyes, looking distressed with a gun in her hand inside her house, made a video call. Through the video call, this woman was showing the other person the state Afghanistan was in. Then, the woman said, 'I'm going to kill myself'. The voice on the other side said, 'No! You're a fighter! We haven't fought so many years to end our lives like this.' The person on the other side was Khalida Popal, the former women's soccer team captain. The woman who made the call was also an Afghan women's soccer team member. Khalida activated the spirit of activism when she said the words, 'We haven't fought for so long . . .' The fact that these women have become soccer player team members in a country like Afghanistan gives you a clear idea of the amount of resistance they have fought against. After that call that day, Khalida knew she had to work very hard in the coming days to get all these women out of Kabul. Khalida was based in Denmark and she had to reach out to everybody she knew—all the influential people—activists, sports people, politicians to get them out of the country. Luckily, a breakthrough happened when help came from Australia. One of the members of parliament in Australia was advocating for them and a local soccer star Craig Fisher reached out to the foreign minister, who also happened to be the minister for foreign affairs and they all together made it possible for these women to get the documents to get out of Afghanistan. Now this was the easy bit. The tougher bit was yet to come.

The question was, 'How can we get these hundred people which included the women's soccer team players and their families all across

Afghanistan to one common meeting point. Khalida directed close to a hundred of them to come to a rendezvous point which was a petrol station about 200 meters away from the airport. The entire group reached the petrol station in their sneakers, track pants, backpacks and covid masks to start their new life and then made their way to the gate. Unfortunately, the gate remained closed. There was no one to open the gate for them. Distressed, they placed a call back to Khalida. This time, Khalida redirected them to another gate but the problem between this gate and the other gate was that the people from the Taliban were there. The people from the Taliban were firing guns in the air, and these were the people that these women were trying to get away from. At that point, they spotted sewage that was leading towards the airport gate. So, they got into the sewage and that's where the trouble began.

There were so many people inside. Elbows were pushing, people started getting exhausted, some vomited, some couldn't breathe properly and fainted. Things became so difficult that a lot of them thought that they were not going to be able to get out. They felt that this was it. This was the best they could do and this was the end. At this juncture, they again called Khalida and even Khalida felt helpless at this time. Around this time, Khalida received close to forty messages and she was losing hope. So she closed her eyes and said, 'I closed my eyes and I told them, you know what, this is a game and we are going to play it. The airport gate is the trophy and we don't give up.' The spirit of sports, the spirit of activism once again lifted their spirits and they persisted and eventually got to the gate. When they got there, there were so many people flashing passports, trying to get the troops who were helping to evacuate people to select them and bring them inside the airport. These women just said two words, "Football. Australian".' That way, the troops knew exactly who they were. They literally picked them up, put them inside the airport and that day, close to eighty-six women along with their family got out of Afghanistan thanks to Khalida.

If you look a little closer, you will realize that these women's identity was built on something they chose. The narrative they told themselves was based on the identity they had chosen. They weren't just Afghan women. They were Afghan soccer players. That was their chosen identity. It was this chosen identity that Khalida spoke to. When they were on the brink of giving up, she spoke about their identity as soccer players. She talked about 'the why' that they believed in. She inspired them to act based on something they held really close to themselves, their identity. When you put in great efforts to a chosen, common identity within your team, it gives birth to a great story which the world talks about. It is the entire mindset that fits within this identity that gives everyone the same lift of energy when they need to come together to achieve a common goal. It is this sports identity that the Afghan women soccer team players had chosen that they had worked towards every single day which gave them the tenacity to be able to get through their entire process of getting out of the country.

The question you have to ask yourself as the leader is, 'What is the team's identity?' and 'What effort am I making towards building that team identity every single day'. Being a great leader is a highly personal journey. If you don't have a good handle on yourself, you won't have a good handle on how to best support your team. No matter what obstacles you face, you first need to get deep with knowing you—your identity, your strengths, your values, your comfort zones, your blind spots, your personality, and your biases. When you fully understand yourself, you will have an inner compass to always guide you to your true north. As you continue to learn and grow, you will build your own arsenal of superpowers.

Think about it

- Do you acknowledge your potential for bias?
- Are you constantly learning about stereotypes to understand how it influences your decisions?
- Are you exposing yourself to different experiences to change the unfamiliar into the familiar?

Chapter 6: Connection: Spark and Sustain Long-lasting Relationships

I define connection as the energy that exists between people when they feel seen, heard, and valued; when they can give and receive without judgment; and when they derive strength and sustenance from the relationship.

—Brené Brown

The fact is, we are social creatures. We thrive in communities and this is one of the reasons why we have a deep-rooted psychological need for social approval. Our brain is hardwired for this social connection. It's even proven to be really good for your wellbeing too. Social approval affects the vagus nerve which starts in your brain stem. It can have the effect of slowing your heart rate and it regulates your heartbeat. When you take time to actually connect with people in your team, and are truly present with them, it naturally boosts engagement. Why? Because people love feeling valued and seen. We all know what it's like when a manager shows a genuine interest in who you are and makes an effort to actually connect with you. You feel valued, appreciated; we know from decades, the worth of research that engaged employees perform better. It is a giant win-win-win.

Building a connection is so important that professional speakers swear by it and use it every time they are speaking to a new audience.

Malcolm Gladwell, author of many bestselling books, goes to an event in India to speak and he starts off his speech by saying,

> 'This is my first time in India but this is not my first experience with India. Up until recently, my father taught at the University of Waterloo in Canada and he always had this stream of brilliant Indian students. These students would always turn up at our place on a Friday or Saturday evening just around dinner time. So when I was growing up, if somebody asked me 'What does Indian culture stand for?', my response would be—the love for learning and the expectation to be fed.'

Now the simple question we have to ask ourselves is why did Malcolm start his speech like that? It's all about connection. He's speaking in India for the first time before he dives into the topic he was meant to talk about. He needs to create that connection and taking time out to do that was really important to do upfront so that his messages later on in his speech would stick with them. The same holds true for leaders who want to connect with their team members.

A chance to communicate is a chance to change the way you connect with people and the way people feel. One of my corporate coaching clients that I was working with, who had to deliver a strategy session in a town hall, asked me to review her agenda. So I asked her to talk me through the agenda of the town hall. She shared her agenda as follows:

1. We start off with strategy
2. We do a poll to find out how people are feeling
3. We give out awards to acknowledge great work that has been done

After giving it a quick look, I suggested a few changes to help her connect better with her team. I asked her, why don't you rearrange the events as follows:

1. Start with the poll to find out how people are feeling. Acknowledge the feelings on the ground as important and let them know you are listening to them.

2. Then, change the mood slightly with celebrations and acknowledging people's great work. This also influences others to put in effort to do the great work because people are most influenced by people like them.

3. Lastly, get into strategy because once you change the state of mind that people are in, you can change the way people behave and once you are able to influence the way people behave, you can drive the right results.

You're doing the same things, except you are placing an emphasis on feelings first and tasks later.

'We human beings are social beings. We come into the world as the result of other's actions. We survive here in dependence on others. Whether we like it or not, there is hardly a moment of our lives when we do not benefit from others' activities. For this reason, it is hardly surprising that most of our happiness arises in the context of our relationships with others'

—the Dalai Lama

In 2008, researchers at the Living Links Center of Emory University did a fascinating study with four pairs of female capuchin monkeys. They found that monkeys got a rush of pleasure from sharing their food with other monkeys. This is how the experiment went:

The researchers allowed one monkey from each pair to choose a token that would either (a) reward only the monkey who had the token with the treat or (b) reward both monkeys in the pair with a treat. The monkeys systematically preferred the pro-social option as long as their partner was familiar, visible, and receiving rewards of equal value. It was clear from the experiment that seeing the other monkey get food was rewarding for the monkeys, and they also observed that the monkeys were more likely to share when they felt a close, personal connection with one another. Deep down, people from all over the world share the basic need for human connection.

You might have heard the popular saying,

'It is not what you know, but who you know that matters.'

This is so true, because it is always people who make the hiring or firing decisions, people who decide who should get promoted, and people who decide who should be invited to important meetings. There has never been a better time to reach out and connect than right now. The dynamic of our society and particularly our economy will increasingly be defined by our interdependence and interconnectivity. In other words, the more everything becomes connected to everything and everyone else, the more we begin to depend on whom and what we're connected with. In the digital era, when the Internet has broken down geographic boundaries and connected hundreds of millions of people and computers around the world, there's no reason to live and work in isolation.

At one financial firm, the senior leaders met at the end of the year to rate the juniors. If a certain manager had worked with you, they would give you points for that. If a manager had interacted with you during a social event, you will get points for that as well. Similarly, if a manager spoke highly of you and recommended you, you would get points for that as well. Eventually, the junior with the most number of accumulated points would get on the fast track for promotion and receive a larger bonus. One thing that the senior leaders realized after running this meeting for a few years was that it was not the smartest or most hardworking person who got access to the fast track. It was the individual who had the most managers praising them behind closed doors. And the ones who fell 'below expectations' were the ones that no one noticed.

Having a support network that you can rely on and confide in is one of the biggest assets you can build while you take on your leadership role. You can't know everything you need to know to be successful. Nobody can. We need the advice and feedback of people we trust to move ahead. That is why first-time mothers instinctively join WhatsApp groups to reach out to other mothers for advice. It is why parents talk to other parents about school, extracurricular activities, social events, dating, and more. It is why the best teams and most successful ones surpass each team member's wildest individual dreams. Experience will not save your job in hard times, nor will hard work or talent. If you need a job, advice, money, help, hope, or a means to make a sale, there's only one surefire fail-safe place to find it—within your extended circle of friends and associates. Each of us now is a brand. Gone are the days where your value as an employee was limited to your loyalty and seniority. In today's fluid economy, you must do the same with your network. It is your relationship with others that is your finest, most credible indicator of who you are and what you have to offer. Nothing else compares.

Behind every great leader, at the base of every great tale of success, you will find an indispensable circle of trusted advisors, mentors, and colleagues. These groups come in all forms and sizes and can be found at every level and in nearly all spheres of both professional and personal life. What they have in common, however, is the unique kind of connection with each other that is known as lifeline relationships. These relationships are quite literally why some people succeed far more than others. That is what I mean by connecting. It is a constant process of meeting new people, giving and receiving help. A network functions precisely because there's recognition of mutual need. There is an implicit understanding that investing time and energy in building personal relationships with the right people will pay dividends.

Moreover, being in an Asian culture, we are much more interdependent in our thinking and values compared to our Western counterparts. Asians are keenly aware of their interconnectedness with others, and tend to understand the 'self' as it is defined by other people. Standing out in the Asian culture is not seen as a positive thing as it highlights individualism over collectivism. Instead, it is seen as something that needs to be fixed. This is best described by a Japanese saying that goes like this:

'The nail that pops out gets hammered back down.'

In such scenarios, it is best to have strong social capital with the people in your network. Each one of us is a leader, manager, parent and entrepreneur seeking answers. All of us work hard at our jobs and careers. We are all leaders in our own lives—with our colleagues, with our children, with our employees, and in our communities. And most of us come up against personal and professional problems that are just too big to solve alone. If you want to be successful as you know you can be, you will need the help of others. When we look at any organization from the outside, all we see is a collection of people but that only tells part of the story. It is the hidden relationships and invisible boundaries surrounding them that are really fascinating and important for you to decipher as a leader. Work would be a miserable activity if the only thing we had to do was work with machines all day.

There's a good chance that you've already experienced the power and potential of strong relationships at some point in your life. Imagine some of the best attributes of the best leaders you have ever met. Leaders who encourage you, give you space to grow, appreciate your efforts, don't micromanage but rather guide your development with wisdom, and leaders who handle your mistakes with firmness, understanding and candor. This could also be your friend or family member who drops everything to be there for you at a critical juncture of your life to ensure you don't fail. Picture that person who took a risk for you and would willingly do it again because of the relationship you both share. Imagine having more of these relationships with your team members and other colleagues in your company. How will these connections benefit you? Where employees once found generosity and loyalty in the companies they worked for, today we find them in a web of our own relationships. It isn't blind loyalty or generosity we once gave to a corporation. It is more of a personal kind of loyalty and generosity that is given to your colleagues, your team, your friends, and your customers.

Sadly, the typical reasoning I get from all my clients when I ask them if they have been actively networking is, 'Where will I find the time for that?' It's true. Once work gets in the way, it can be very hard to meet new people, especially with restrictions by governments to limit the spread of COVID-19. So why not start with the people you work with? If the idea of meeting new people makes you break out into a sweat, fret not. It can be a challenge to hold a conversation with a stranger at work when you don't know how to carry the conversation to a proper landing. Even I have experienced the nerves and I know for a fact that all you need is getting used to it. It is natural to get stuck in your own head, thinking about the very thing you just blurted out.

Was I not supposed to know that? Why is there an awkward pause in this conversation? Is this person really busy constantly checking his phone or just not that interested in this conversation? Building confidence and overcoming anxiety are part and parcel of building long term relationships. I like to think of this relationship as a flight that is waiting to take off. Prepare for takeoff, gather momentum and start cruising.

Prepare for takeoff

Spectacular achievement is always preceded by spectacular preparation.
—Unknown

Some companies put a lot of effort into bringing employees together outside of the office. It might be a happy hour, or a team picnic, or an overseas retreat. While such events can be productive if people on your team really want them, it is important to remember that you will mostly get to know your teammates better in the day-to-day grind of getting work done as opposed to a one-off team-bonding event. The best time to bond with your teammates is during an off-peak period, where the pressure of deadlines is low and you can take time out to incorporate new activities. Simple activities like going on a walk or meeting each other's families can have a big impact. When management introduces these kinds of events, it might feel obligatory and forced. Since you are already spending a good amount of time with your colleagues, make it a point to keep aside some time to build relationships.

Imagine you are waiting alone for the lift in your office building in the process of heading out for lunch and someone joins you in the wait. They then ask you an obvious question, 'Out for lunch?' with a smile on their face. You've just found a lunch buddy. This is all it takes to build a connection at work. Based on research by Dr Gottman, a marriage expert, these subtle gestures are what he calls 'bids' which he defines as requests for human connection. They are clues for us to pick up and act upon. According to Gottman, couples who stay married tend to have an acute sense of observing their partner's bids while responding positively to it. The couples who end up in divorce are the ones that tend to miss out or reject their partner's bids. Building strong relationships is about acknowledging others' presence and showing that you care. Expressing appreciation for someone who held the lift longer for you to get in is sometimes all it takes. In order for you to build strong relationships with your team members, you must be prepared for the takeoff. As the leader, you hold more responsibility in the organization. As such, it is advisable for you to take the initiative to reach out to your team members and people in your organization. Whom you meet, how you meet them, and what they think of you after your meeting should not be left to chance.

Before you meet with any new people that you are thinking of meeting up with, you have to research who they are and what they do. You have to find out their hobbies, their goals, and general information about them. You want to know what this individual is like as a human being, what he feels strongly about, and what his proudest achievements are. When you are informed enough to step comfortably into their world and talk knowledgeably, their appreciation will be tangible. Moreover, doing research these days is easy.

Heading over to a meeting without googling someone is simply unacceptable. It gives you relevant information and a sense of how active the person is online and how much information they share. LinkedIn also showcases how you are connected to them and what groups they have joined. Read their work history and summary info carefully. It usually reveals what they're most proud of accomplishing professionally. Your goal in such meetings is to transform what could be a forgettable encounter into a blossoming friendship.

Start with an Observation

If you are planning to connect with someone within your office perimeters, find an excuse to kickstart the conversation. Whenever you have a meeting, use the initial few minutes before the meeting to talk to whoever that has arrived early. You can pull any topic you want out of the air, whether it is the weather, or about work, or about their weekend plans. The key is to prepare some preset topics beforehand so that you don't find yourself grappling for topics after initiating the conversation. Keep a lookout for different moments during the working day where people are typically waiting for something. This is usually prevalent before meetings, while waiting in queue for the lift, or while in queue for lunch and sometimes even when you bump into your colleague while heading to work or heading back home from work. Reaching out to individuals to have conversations will make them feel a sense of belonging and show that you care, remember and value their presence. Above all, when you reach out to them, it makes it easier for them to carry the conversation. Once you get to know the people in your team and department really well, you can leverage their connections to get introduced to others with their help. When requesting an introduction, show your homework, get straight to the point, and have a clear call to action. For instance, you can use a template like this:

> Hi Bruce,
> It was great bumping into you the other day. How did your meeting go? I am wondering if you could introduce me to Stephanie from your department. I'm working on a research project that she might have some insights on and I saw that you are already connected with her on LinkedIn. If you would be open to making an intro, let me know if you need anything from my end to make this easier for you. If I caught you at a bad time, no worries—just let me know either way.
> Best,
> Johnson

Once your contact agrees to connect you with their contact, you can ask them how they would prefer to be connected. The best is to have a three-way coffee introduction to showcase the strength of your relationship with your contact. If that is not possible, an email or WhatsApp group introduction would also suffice. Something as simple as this will do:

> *Dear Stephanie,*
> *Please meet a dear friend and colleague of mine, Johnson, who is interested in speaking with you about his research project. Hope you both get a chance to connect!*
> *All the best,*
> *Bruce*

Once both parties initiate the conversation, it is safe to set aside a proper time and place for the conversation. To avoid unnecessary back and forth, I suggest coming up with three time slots that are available for them to pick and if none of them work, ask them to suggest three time slots as possible alternatives. Once a preferred time is fixed, send a calendar invite to confirm the meeting. Also make sure you thank the person for taking time out for the meeting once you have met them.

One thing to avoid once you build connections is to stop keeping score. You cannot amass a network of connections without introducing such connections to others with equal fervour. The more people you help, the more help you will have. It is the same phenomenon that works in top social networking sites. The more people access it and use it, the more valuable the network becomes. In an interdependent world, flattened organizations seek out strategic alliances at every turn. Win–win has become the necessary reality in a networked world.

Gather Momentum

The key to sending invitations that get accepted when contacting people outside our network is to make our invitation customized. Most people do this poorly because they don't realize the power it has in eliciting a response. People like people who are similar to them, so the more you can enhance the similarities when reaching out, the higher your chances of getting that meeting. A good litmus test to ensure you are customizing the email is to ask, 'Would my email still make sense if I sent it to the wrong person.' If you answered yes, then the email is not customized enough, and there is a high chance they might see your email as spam. Make it as easy as possible for others to say yes to you. Building your network means you have to make it a priority to be around people. If you are working on-site, stay close to your team. Make it a point to walk by people's desks and say hello. Be proactive in asking people if they would like to order lunch through you, since you're stepping outside to get some takeaway food anyway. You can do this even when you are planning to grab coffee because people appreciate these small gestures that show your sincerity.

If you are working remotely, make sure you are seen regularly by having at least one friend who is working on-site. In this situation, you must have the right connections to give you updates on what is going on at the ground level and have someone advocate for you even when you aren't in the room. Make it a point to have as many video calls as possible so that people associate with you for more than just your voice. Take initiatives in organizing a few important meetings, staff retreats, and running employee resources groups. When you are working remotely, you must put in extra effort and energy to ensure others notice you. You can do this by being more active in virtual meetings by responding first to questions, offering more status updates than you would have done working on-site. If you get opportunities to work with different people, sign up for it. Meet people outside your immediate circle to grow your network. This gives you the opportunity to strike up new conversations with others and get comfortable in having small talk. Cross team projects and initiatives can be really useful to grow your network within the organization. You can kick start the conversation with work topics and transition into non-work topics such as, 'What do you usually do when you're not working?'.

If your coworkers are organizing social events, consider joining. A lawyer friend I had interviewed told me about how someone who started at the same time as him ended up with more mentors and doing interesting projects because he spent his time meeting people within the organization. It wasn't because the person worked harder. It was because he met all the right people during the social events. If there is a work event, consider showing up even if it is for just a short while. The more you appear in these events, the more your co-workers develop familiarity in seeing you at these events. That ensures you can be invited every time an event like this happens. The opposite applies as well where if you are absent for too many events in a row, people start getting used to your absence and don't remember to invite you to future events. One thing to note about social events; if alcohol is involved, remember this is still a work event. You still have to behave professionally in such social settings. You don't want to end up drinking too much. A drink or two can act as a social lubricant. If you let go of your limits, the number of things that can go wrong are countless. I've had clients share with me incidents of their colleagues who vomitted at a party from drinking too much, some who slapped a police officer while intoxicated, office couches that had to be removed because it was clear that people had sex on it. The emotional trauma and broken families that arise from too much intoxication is not worth the trouble and is a surefire way to destroy relationships. If you don't want to consume alcohol at all, tell them you have an early morning to prepare for and keep repeating it until they realize there's no point in persuading you to drink. It's better to be on the safe side.

If events are limited due to pandemic restrictions, consider connecting with people within your organization on LinkedIn. You can do this without being introduced. What you want to ensure is that you have a good read of the person's profile before you connect with them. When it comes to building a relationship from an online space, it is vital that you learn as much as you can about the person before you initiate contact. When sending the invitation to connect, remember to include something about the person in your message so that they know you are sincere about connecting. Whether it is a common friend, common hobby or event, make sure you mention it in the message when you connect with them. A personalized message goes a much longer distance than a basic one. Most people don't even send a message, they simply click the connect button and wait for the other party to accept. When searching for new people to add on LinkedIn, you want to check if the person is active on that platform in the first place. While browsing through their profile, you can see their 'recent activity' which can tell you when they were last active. You can tell if this person is highly engaged with the LinkedIn community or if they barely hop on once every month to check for any new updates. A person who is highly engaged will be seen liking, commenting and sharing content on the platform. All of these content pieces or actions are doorways to start off a conversation. You can comment on their posts or respond to their comments on someone else's post for them to get a sense of familiarity before reaching out to connect. If you haven't recently taken the time to connect to people this week, to connect to people on LinkedIn, take out two hours on your calendar this week to send out personalized invites to as many people in your network as you have time for.

Once you have connected, it is about highlighting the similarities you have with one another. Establishing rapport comes from increasing similarities and decreasing differences. The more the other person finds something similar, the more invested they become in the conversation. Even a topic as basic as getting sick works. Commonalities are a quick way to build compatibility. Talking about a topic that both sides are familiar with makes it easier for everyone to pull new topics into the conversation. When you are meeting with people who are in your cold network, it is critical that you read up about them beforehand to prepare yourself with topics to talk about. Showing up with a list of questions to ask them also demonstrates that you've done your homework. Asking questions shows your curiosity toward the other person and also gives them a chance to share more about themselves. It also allows you to reflect on their answers and share your own stories that relate to the same point. It also lets people know that you are a good listener and having conversations with you is a worthwhile activity. Nobody likes to be stuck with someone who is giving a monologue and nobody wants to feel like they are talking to a wall. Try to introduce more details about yourself as the conversation deepens so that the other person also feels comfortable doing the same. While in conversation, put your phone away in your bag or in your pocket. It is one of the best ways you can indicate to the other party that your attention is completely on them. If you must multitask due to some urgent work, share with them about what you are going to do before you go ahead and do it. Sometimes, all it takes is a simple explanation to let the other party feel respected. 'Oh, I've gotten an important email/text that I need to attend to. Let me quickly send off a reply because this is urgent.'

If you've ever observed a couple on their date at a café, you might notice two very different things. Either they're sitting the same way, leaning towards each other, almost like they're mirroring their body language or their body language is completely disconnected. If this was a couple on the first date, which one do you think will progress to the second date? The one with matching, connected body language or the one with disconnected body language? This phenomenon is called the 'Chameleon Effect'. When people are genuinely connected or on the same 'wavelength', they tend to be like chameleons and adapt to each other's tone of voice, pace of speech, and even their body language. If you want to build stronger rapport with the person you are in conversation with, consider mirroring their body language. Sit in a similar fashion, almost as if you are a mirror reflection of the other person. This helps them open up. To take it one step further, you can even use the same words they use and mirror it often to signal similarity with the other party. Bouncing the same body language and words that the other person uses often, indicates you are in sync with the other person. If you would like to test the strength of your rapport, adopt the other person's body language first for five minutes and then drastically change up your body posture in a natural manner. You could cross your legs or lean in towards your right side. If the person you are in rapport with feels uncomfortable, they too will adjust their body posture to adopt something that mirrors you.

Once the meeting comes to an end, it is important that you capture all the information you had about the person into a document. Documenting this information will help you in the long run, because it will remind you of the details of the last conversation you had with this person. Most times, people meet once and then leave it at that. However, to remain top of mind, it is important for you to stay in touch with them every quarter. The successful organization and management of the information you collect that makes connecting flourish is vital. Keeping tabs on the people you met, the people you want to know, and doing all the homework that will help you develop strong and lasting relationships with others can create a problem with information overload. It can be overwhelming when you do not organize everything you know well. This is where you have to understand that it is not about collecting the information, it is about filtering it. The problem isn't in information overload, it is in filter failure. Our challenge these days is to figure out amongst the mass of connections we have built, which ones matter the most. The people who build social platforms know this and are getting better at helping you filter out the noise. You can do this by creating documents that organize your contacts into people you have met and people you want to meet. Then, you can add columns to organize information such as where they are based, industries and companies they work in, activities they are involved in, interests they pursue passionately, and associations or groups that they are part of. It goes without saying that you should have their mobile number and email contact and social media profile links to stay connected at all times. If you really want to take this to the next level, take a leaf out of Harvey Mackay's philosophies. Harvey Mackay is the CEO of his own sales and training company, and in his training programs, he highly advocates the philosophy of having critical information about the people you are working with. Granted, you may not be a salesperson but the critical skill you need from a leadership perspective is linked to working with people. Skills like persuasion, influence, and being assertive will only work wonders when you have enough data points about the individual. Mackay created 66 data points to help him generate more conversational topics with people he liked to be around which allowed him to connect with his stakeholders better. This is where a Microsoft Excel document becomes very useful. If you would like to get a Mackay 66 template to use for yourself, head over to www.vivekiyyani.com/free to make a copy.

When it comes to adding names of people you want to meet, it is merely a matter of looking in the right place. Trade magazines usually talk about the influential people who have insights about the industry they are in. Connecting with such influencers always makes it easier to widen your network exponentially. If you happen to read about someone who fits into the bill of people you want to meet, add their names to your list before you make your move to meeting them one day. Newspapers and magazines also have a number of lists of top influencers in various industries and functions. You not only want to know the players who are recognized as the top thirty under thirty or top forty under forty, but be associated with these people as part of your network. Don't worry about connecting to these people immediately.

It is more important to map out who you need to meet to build a strong network before you actually set out to do so.

Start out by reaching out to people whom you have already met before, but might have lost touch along the way. They include relatives, friends of relatives, all of your spouse's relatives and connections, current colleagues, ex-colleagues, members of professional and social organizations, current and former customers and clients, parents of your children's friends, neighbours past and present, people you went to school with, former teachers and employers, people you socialize with, and connections that you have met before in some form on social media.

Usually, enough changes would have happened in one's life every ninety days to get a new update. Make sure you reconnect with them and ask them out for lunch to swap updates. Sometimes they may have left their organization to start a new job, or they could have started their own side hustle; some might have gotten married and started a family, or some may have pursued further education. The possibilities are endless and it shouldn't be surprising to see people to have many updates every quarter. Relationships aren't built from singular conversations. They are built from multiple interactions over many weeks and months. Even before meeting up with them, you can add value to them in three ways.

1. Introduce Them to Someone They Might Benefit From

If you made that document after meeting with a person, you would have an idea of what is going on in their lives. Asking questions like 'What's the next big thing for you' and 'What's the biggest challenge you're facing regarding that' can reveal the exact pain points that are relevant to this person. With this information in mind, you can introduce the right person to them to add value to their lives. If they are getting married and are in search of a good caterer, photographer, or venue, and you happen to know someone who might be able to help them out, make the introduction. Connect people to help those in your network and soon enough, you will see many people reaching out to you for introductions. You will become the center of influence because you know people. Moreover, when you are introducing someone who provides a service, do not make the mistake of only introducing one party. If you know three wedding photographers, introduce all three instead of one because it reduces the risk of tarnishing your name. In the event you introduced only one photographer, and they hired him for the wedding but he ended up botching the job for their wedding, it is your reputation that suffers because of this. Instead, introducing three potential photographers that you are in touch with allows them to pick the person who is best suited for their requirements and it reduces the pressure. No one can fault you for the introduction because you gave them more than one introduction.

2. Buy Them a Meaningful Gift They Will Appreciate

Another way you can add value to your network is to go back to your notes to see what this individual spoke passionately about. Is this person a big fan of a musician? Do they love art? Are they into sports? Or do they collect certain types of books? If you asked the right questions and listened keenly to their answers, you would know what they fancy. This makes it easier for you to surprise them with a gift either on their birthdays or on occasions like Christmas or Thanksgiving. In fact, if you would like to really surprise them, send it to them randomly and let them know that this 'gift' reminded you of them. A gift with a handwritten note is rare to come across these days and it will really make a strong impression on their minds. Of course, it is worth mentioning that giving out gifts with an expectation of some favours in return will be sniffed out immediately. If the person you are talking to is the head of procurement and you are a vendor who wants to do projects with this organization, you stand the risk of putting that person in trouble if you send them gifts before or after the tender is awarded. Be clear in this aspect. Check in with the person if they are okay with receiving gifts and ensure they are comfortable with it. The best way to do this is by asking them or testing it out with small inexpensive but meaningful gifts.

Ken Honda, author of *Happy Money*, shares a story of how he became super successful in his twenties as an accounting consultant. He divided his entire clientele base into two groups: one that he gave gifts to and one that he didn't. He always brought something whenever he went to meet them. Gifts like Japanese herbal tea or a book that was cheap. Within 6 months, he got so many referrals from the members of the group that he constantly gifted without asking for anything in return. He highly recommends everybody to start giving more, just something a little extra, to show your appreciation. The more you give, the more you automatically attract. He also mentions that people with the radiance of appreciation have a different level of energy which often attracts more people to connect with you. What you appreciate, appreciates.

3. Invite Them to an Event That They Will Benefit From

If gifts are not an option, you could invite them to events that they might appreciate. Whether it is a wine-tasting event for wine enthusiasts, or a rock band concert for avid fans, or a seminar on a specific topic that is of interest to them, inviting people to events is one of the best ways you can stay engaged with them. When you give them those free tickets to something they enjoy, you get to impress them and at the same time engage with them during the event. It allows you to build the relationship to a deeper level. It gives you a chance to share relevant articles, videos, podcast episodes, or newsletters to signal to them that you have been thinking about your last conversation. It allows you to weave multiple topics together into the conversation. Soon enough, you can shift your conversations about the past and present, and focus more on the future. If you would like to work together with this person, you can try saying, 'If you are in need of an extra pair of hands, please keep me in mind.'

When it comes to leveraging your network, the biggest sin is to become invisible. It means you should always be reaching out to others over breakfast or lunch to continuously connect with people. In building a network, it never ever disappears. While it is hard work to build a network, it doesn't have to mean you work longer than you want to. It shouldn't feel like you are slogging all day without seeing any real returns. Connecting properly means you are building relationships and it is a fun process. When you find yourself wanting to meet more people and having less time, invite all of them to the same lunch or dinner and connect with all of them at the same time. There are bound to be synergies that will allow them to benefit personally or professionally as well. If you want to spend more time with someone in particular, ask them to come 45 minutes earlier to enjoy the personal time together. It is also important to observe during such combined meetings and look out for the chemistry between people. Some get along well with others instantly, others take a bit of time to warm up. Trust your instincts before you invite them together and let fate take its course from there.

Make it a point to include others in whatever you are doing. It is a win-win-win situation for all. The more people you involve, the more you are effectively multi-tasking by growing your network. The bigger your network, the more attractive it becomes. It is like a muscle, the more you work it, the more use it will be to you. Friendship is created out of the quality of time spent between two people. Most people often mistake it as the quantity of time that they need to spend together in order to form a strong relationship. It is what you do together that matters, not how often you meet. This is why it is important to stay organized so that you can pay special attention to where you're most comfortable and what activities you enjoy. This will automatically bring out the best in you and make connecting a fun process.

What about Vulnerability?

This is a question I get asked a lot, and to be completely honest, it is about understanding that vulnerability does not work like a switch. It is not something that you can turn on and be completely vulnerable about everything. Think of it as a spectrum, and inch forward carefully because you don't want your vulnerability to backfire on you. When you open yourself up to others by sharing some of your struggles when things didn't work out, you come across as more human and relatable. This also makes you very likable. When you disclose stories and open up to the people in your team, it encourages others to reciprocate by making them feel far more comfortable to also open up. Psychologists call it the 'Disclosure Reciprocity' which is the adult version of 'I'll tell you my secret if you tell me yours'. It is known to build trust and empathy and it goes to the core of connection. However, it is entirely possible to screw things up by being too vulnerable, especially in the initial stages of the working relationship with your team members. There's a way to ease into sharing vulnerability stories by sharing things that do not reflect upon your competency as a leader.

Share Your Scar, Not Your Wound

Scars are a representation of the battles that have been fought, and lessons that have been learnt from it. It is a reminder of what we went through, and because it doesn't hurt when you touch it, it is an indication that you have moved on from it—whatever that caused the scar. Sharing the stories behind the scar is a powerful way to draw your people into the lessons you have learnt along the way. However, some experiences leave a nasty wound that takes much longer to heal. Sharing those stories when the wound hasn't fully healed can be detrimental to you and might come back to hurt you. Simply put, if you haven't healed completely from the experiences, it might not be a good idea to share them in the name of vulnerability.

On the 4 February 2014, Satya Nadella was appointed as the third CEO of Microsoft and on that day, he wrote a letter to his employees. In that letter, there was one line in which he said, 'I buy more books than I can read and sign up for more courses than I can finish.' That line is a classic example of vulnerability without having to share anything personal. Great leaders already do this, especially in situations where they don't know exactly what to say. They are being vulnerable when they say, 'I don't know, but I would like to learn' or 'I don't know, but let's figure it out together'. There is no need to unnecessarily exploit vulnerability with personal stories to create strong connections with the people on your team. Too much of anything can create opportunities for vulnerability to backfire so tread with caution.

Leave No Room for Shame and Embarrassment

This should be common sense but it's pretty amazing how many leaders (consciously and otherwise) shame people publicly when they don't know something which they thought they should. Dr Brené Brown, author of *I Thought It was Just Me* shares a story of being shamed when she was invited to a dinner. When they went there, the host served an appetizer which was in a large, silver bowl with some beans in it. Brené Brown had never seen those beans before so she thought her host wanted her to open up the beans so that they could be prepared for dinner. Out of curiosity, she looked at the bowl, then looked at the host, and then she asked, 'What is it?' The host looked back at her and said, 'What do you mean what is it?! They're Edamame beans! Haven't you ever had them? Have you never eaten Japanese food?' At this stage, Brené Brown started to feel a little bit of shame for not knowing about the appetizer which was probably common knowledge. To make things worse, the host went around to tell other guests in the party that Brené had never had Edamame beans. Two weeks later, Brené looked up the beans and even became a fan of it. One day, when her student visited her in her office, he noticed the beans and asked her the same question, 'What is that?' and despite being the victim to shaming, she did the exact thing the host did to her at the event to the student. In other words, she shifted the shame. She turned around to the student and asked, 'Haven't you tried these? They're Edamame beans. I can't believe you didn't know what these are. These beans are really healthy. They're the new superfood. You must try them!' Upon reflection, Brené says that although she didn't mean to shame her student, she did it because of class. Knowing more about Japanese food and culture was associated with being high-class in her mind and class is known to be a huge shame trigger. Brené wanted to show her student that she had class, and inadvertently, ended up shaming her because of it.

Today, organizations are going through a lot. There's a lot of new things coming in like digital transformation, artificial intelligence, automation, smart initiatives, and new ways of working, etc. There's a lot that your people won't know, and it might be even harder for the older generations to pick up on these changes that seem to be happening at alarming speeds. The choice—whether to reinforce the shame, shift the shame or disregard the shame—is completely yours. It is the culture that you can choose to bring people in your team closer together. But how do you disregard shame?

Once when I was sharing an exciting idea that I had learnt recently with my close friend, I mentioned the word 'Ted Talk'. My friend turned around and asked me, 'What is a Ted Talk?' Rather than saying 'Don't you know what a Ted Talk is?' I said to her, 'Oh, right, yes . . . don't worry, you don't do research on such topics. There is no reason why you should know what a Ted Talk is. I watch Ted Talks to broaden my mind about interesting ideas . . . I use it also as a form of research.' Then, I went on to show her some videos on https://www.Ted.com to help her understand what it was all about. It's always easy to name and shame people, but it goes against you when you're working to build stronger connections together. Do not reinforce shame. Disregard it completely and provide a safe space to those who work with you to the extent where they are no longer afraid of asking 'stupid questions'. It will help people open up to you effortlessly.

When we are truly passionate about something, it's contagious. Our passion draws people to who we are and what we care about. Others respond by letting their guard down. It is astonishing how much you can find out about one another when you are doing something you both enjoy. If you haven't already, make a list of things you are most passionate about. Use your passions as a guide to which activities and events you should be seeking out. Use them to engage new and old contacts. If you love badminton, take your team out for a badminton game or invite them to join you in watching a tournament. Your passions and the events you organize around your passion will create deeper levels of intimacy. Pay attention to matching the event to the particular relationship you are trying to build. Make an informal list of activities that you can use to stay in touch with your business and personal friends.

Here are some quick ideas you can use to engage your network:

1. A cup of coffee in fifteen minutes. It is quick and it is out of the office or home, wherever you are working from. It is one of the best ways to meet someone new. Be sure to communicate why the fifteen minutes will be valuable for the other party as well to get their buy-in.

2. Go to conferences near your location and let people in your list know that you will be in the area. They could either join you for the conference or just drop in for lunch to have a short catch up.

3. Invite your connections to a workout run or a hobby like chess or gardening.

4. Invite someone to a special event such as a book launch, or a concert of your favorite band. The event is made more special when you get the tickets and ask them to join you.

5. Invite them to a dinner party at home. Dinner parties are the best ways you can invite all the important people in your life and connect them to people they haven't met yet. In such scenarios, invite more people you know and fewer people whom you are merely acquainted with. The whole idea is to get your network to feel like they grew their network by attending your party.

6. Volunteering is also a powerful way to meet with people. Connecting with volunteers who are passionate about a cause that you are as passionate about will make it easy for you to create a strong connection.

Start Cruising

Remember, once you get organized, focused and disciplined in developing this contact database, there is no one who is truly out of reach. The strategies we discuss in this chapter don't only apply in the work context, but to life in general as well. The first time for anything feels uncomfortable, but it gets easier with practice. The second, third, and fourth times will be easier than the previous time. Before long, the stranger that you got connected to through LinkedIn can be the one who vouches for you to be a part of an inter-departmental project within your organization. He can be a familiar face, acquaintance or supportive ally depending on the efforts you put into the relationship. The earlier you set up your own brain trust of important people, the more opportunities you will attract to yourself. The rule in life that has unprecedented power is that the individual who knows the right people, for the right reasons, and utilizes the power of these relationships becomes the person with influence. When your day is fuelled by passion and full of interesting people to share it with, connecting will become less of a chore and very soon, you will find yourself cruising comfortably while building your network.

Think about it

- What are your gifts, talents, and strengths?
- Where do you struggle the most?
    - Starting a strong relationship?
    - Sustaining and staying in touch to keep your relationships warm?
    - Letting go of relationships that are harmful and holding you back
- What are some ways you have cultivated relationships so far? How did you manage to build strong relationships with the people you are in touch with?

Chapter 7: Candour: Making Difficult Conversations Easy

Being a foreigner for the most part of my childhood and teenage years, working as a student was a relatively new concept to me. It actually surprised me that some of my classmates would take up full-time jobs at the tender age of sixteen to earn some side income. The narrative that I was fed back then was to completely focus my attention and time on studying well and getting good grades. Working part-time was seen as a distraction and for the most part, I didn't see the need for it either. As a result, the first 'work experience' I had was when I joined the national service in Singapore and enlisted for two years. I started out as a recruit, got into leadership school to train and graduated as a sergeant and I was posted back to Basic Military School (BMT) where the recruits would come for a three-month indoctrination, from civilian to soldier. This time, as I headed back as a Sargent, I had responsibilities and I was in-charge of training and taking care of the young soldiers. This is where I observed the challenges of a leader who faced pressure from the top as well as from the bottom. It was also the time where I had my first experience of a 'toxic workplace'.

Being in the army, the rules are way different from a corporate atmosphere. Every sentence from the top included three to four words of vulgarities and the rationale for such language was that 'it toughens you up'. In such environments, it is to be expected. Even as a leader, you are not excused from the tough love that is showered upon you. The entire leadership in the 'company' that I was part of believed that humiliation was a great motivator to change behaviour. Any mistakes you make will result in public humiliation in front of the recruits and other leaders within the company. Because of this, everyone was on their toes and the attitude they had towards work became very selfish. Even though we were brothers-in-arms, all we cared about was to ensure we did not have to face the brunt and verbal diarrhea of a pissed off officer. Hence, a common phrase that was used to encapsulate this behaviour was coined. If you've been through national service before, you probably have heard this term before. Essentially it means to save yourself instead of trying to save others. The term, as we knew it, is called 'cover backside', and it means the same thing literally. When you end up in a toxic workplace, that becomes your key motivator. To pass by each day without being screamed at or humiliated in public. The only relief I had while serving my two years there was that I wasn't alone in bearing the brunt. Everyone got their fair share and learned from it. Was it effective? Yes. Did it make me respect my leaders though? Definitely not. My seniors definitely had the rank and the technical knowledge, but I wasn't quite sure if they knew anything about being an inspirational leader.

It was not until years later, did I get to see the value of giving feedback when it is really required. When I started out on my own and hired part-timers, I made a mental note to ensure that my style of managing them should not reflect what my leaders in the army did. In trying to avoid the mistakes that they made, I made a very different set of mistakes on my own. Instead of telling people they needed to buck up when their work wasn't good enough, I merely played down their faults. I avoided confrontation in fear of losing them as my trainers. In a gig economy, it is all about relationships and since no one is tied down to any company, a simple conflict was all it took to lose out on talent. I failed to create a working climate where feedback was delivered in an inspirational way instead of in a derogatory manner like my previous bosses. I naively assumed that if I didn't address the issues at hand on time, they would automatically go away on their own. Going down hard on someone wasn't something I wanted, but at the same time, not correcting the mistakes my freelancers made was affecting the business. It was only after a few mishaps that I realized I had to step in and bring up the mistakes to their awareness level. Procrastinating on this matter didn't help. That was when I realized that criticism and appreciation both go hand in hand to develop a strong and cohesive team. In order to do this right, you need to build the relationship with your team to the point where there is mutual trust. At the heart of being an inspirational leader is having a good relationship with the people you work with.

One of the hardest things that Millennials and Gen Zs struggle with is having difficult conversations with people. There is a lack of courage in social interactions especially when it comes to difficult topics that need to be talked about. It is a skill that is severely lacking in many and the way many cope with it is by ghosting. Ghosting is a phenomenon predominantly seen amongst the younger generation. When they have decided that they want to break up with someone or if they don't want to be friends anymore after a bad conflict, they literally just stop responding. No more responses to text, they don't answer phone calls, they may unfriend or block you on social media and simply disappear from your life. So in romantic relationships, instead of having a break up, they just ghost. It is the greatest act of cowardice to not have a confrontation and the worst part is for the person who is on the receiving end of it. The victim's initial reaction is panic. They think something must have happened to the person who has ghosted them. Then, when they log on to social media, they realize that no one is in danger, but they have been ghosted, unfriended or blocked. This then makes the victim wonder, 'What have I done wrong? Is it something I did?' which completely destroys their self-esteem. Their desire to get answers goes unanswered and it becomes so destructive to the victim. Having a big fight and getting some closure is better than ghosting. Ghosting is an act of cowardice and indicates a lack of skillset.

I've personally experienced being ghosted by some of my freelance associate trainers who completely disappeared from my radar even when they were expected to turn up for a training assignment. There is no apology, let alone an explanation of what happened. The reason?

They are afraid of saying things as it is. They are afraid of being in a difficult conversation. They know they screwed up, but they don't know how to make things better again. And it can be for the silliest of reasons—such as 'I overslept'—but the fear of being confronted combined with the lack of consequence from ghosting (because they are not bound as a gig worker unlike in a full-time job) makes them choose ghosting over having difficult conversations.

If you are part of a large organization, it is nearly impossible to have a relationship with everyone. However, you can get to know the people in your team really well. These relationships are core to your job as a leader. They determine if you can fulfill your responsibilities of giving guidance, motivating your team members, and drive results through collaboration. There is a virtuous cycle between your relationships and your responsibilities. You strengthen your relationships by learning the best ways to guide others, by putting the right people in the right roles, and by achieving results together that are not possible to achieve individually. Your relationship with your team members directly affects the relationships they have with their direct reports. It influences your team's culture and your ability to build trusting, human connections with the people who directly report to you. The best leaders give feedback clearly and frequently. Sadly, many don't have this routine at all. Even when there are areas for improvement, many don't take out the time to give feedback because they are usually loaded with many other priorities fighting for their attention. Much of the feedback that comes from leaders can be gleaned from offhand remarks and body language as opposed to formal performance reviews. Feedback can be given directly or indirectly in verbal and non-verbal manners. Add culture into the mix and it becomes a lot more complicated to give and receive feedback. What you say might not be what they interpret and understand. The failure of leaders to confront and deal with conflict successfully is evident throughout our businesses, governments, and schools. Plagued by the inability of leaders to leverage the opportunities that conflict offers, a vast majority of our institutions, and our broader social realm, lack this critical component of leadership. As a result, the people and organizations they serve do not perform at the levels they are capable of. The cultures of their organizations fail to develop in a healthy manner and the people in them never feel safe and empowered. Show me a leader that struggles to confront conflict and I will show you the biggest elephant in the room. To be truly successful, leaders must stop avoiding and misusing conflict. Conflict can be a true source of influence and power which can benefit careers, reputations and legacies. It is a source of critical and creative thinking that drives the innovation and change you are responsible and accountable for leading. To practice candor and confront effectively, you need to be aware of the personal risks and fears that keep you from actively addressing the elephants in the room. It is necessary to develop the ability to address your own internal conflicts and not let them become your Achilles heel. The most powerful leaders are paid as much because they pretty much have difficult conversations in difficult situations all day every day. That is the bread and butter of leadership and you must start exercising your muscles to treat a difficult conversation as a learning opportunity rather than something to avoid.

Harvard professor Frances Frei shares a story in her TED Talk when she was an executive on loan at Uber to change the culture of the organization. It was a well-known fact that Uber went through a phase where the work culture had become really toxic. Frances shares the story of a female employee who asked a male employee 'Would you stay back late with me today to finish this project?' The male employee turns around and says, 'Yes, I will. If you sleep with me.' He then skips a beat and says, 'Oh, just kidding!' The point Frances made was that if you have to say 'Just kidding' after just a second of having said something inappropriate, you are very well aware that the comment you made is at risk of being tagged inappropriate or unwelcomed. This is where candor comes in. Quite often in organizations, we just tell people 'This is inappropriate'. What you have to do is to create an opportunity for them to develop new skills to respond. In such situations where someone makes a comment, 'Yes, I will. If you sleep with me' or 'Just kidding!', you have to use candor and say, 'That sounded super inappropriate. Can we try that again?' This time, the person who made the joke has to come up with the right way to respond. By practicing candor, you are creating layers of new responses and changing the culture of your organization. Don't just tell people what they said is inappropriate, tell them to try again and be the role model for your team members who look up to you as their leader.

Since feedback can get confusing for the recipient if they don't understand the subtle nuances, it is important for the leader to master the art of giving feedback and having difficult conversations with candor.

	Verbal	Non-Verbal
Direct	Blunt Opinions	Blunt Actions
Indirect	Subtle Hints	Passive Aggressive behaviour

Subtle Hints

Subtle hints are a form of giving feedback to people who struggle with the idea of receiving feedback. Even if you may not like what you see in terms of output from your direct report, you struggle to convey this to them directly. Even if you do indicate mildly that things could be better, the feedback ends up being very ambiguous to the other party and they might not think of it as feedback. Lukewarm approvals, gentle suggestions and anxious questions are examples of subtle hints. They are mild in nature and do not indicate any strong disapproval to the other party in the conversation. It is usually a diluted version of a potent feedback that could help the individual if they make the changes. A lot of self-censorship happens when leaders struggle to give feedback. This is bad for the leader as well as the direct report that they want better output from. Neither does the direct report realize that their work is shoddy nor does he work on improving simply because he is unaware of the problem at hand. Some individuals, especially personality profiles that prefer to keep the harmony in the team, tend to avoid conflict at all costs. A friend of mine whom I interviewed regarding this told me of an incident where his manager was super sweet during his internship and had a bottom-up approach to leadership. She would always ask for his opinion and be very gentle in sharing some changes that she wanted from him. Her sentences would start with 'How about we try . . .' or 'Is everything okay? Do you have any updates for me?' It was all good until he got his review which really became a shocker. She decided to let go of him within the first month while the other interns continued to stay on for their internship and he found it difficult to connect the dots. Leaders who don't give direct feedback verbally do not realize the consequences of avoiding a responsibility they must take ownership of.

Blunt Opinions

The direct opposite of subtle hints is being overly vocal about what they feel. They don't just think the thoughts, they verbalize it too, sometimes without really considering how the other party might feel. Sometimes this is good because it nubs the issue in the bud instantly but sometimes, it can touch a raw nerve and can potentially and unnecessarily blow up into something bigger than it actually is. While subtle hints are hard to interpret, blunt opinions can be hurtful. Leaders who are used to verbalizing their thoughts tend to knowingly or unknowingly humiliate their colleagues in front of others. Saying things like, 'This report is a piece of crap' or 'Please get out of my face' are comments that no one enjoys hearing. In a panel discussion that I was part of on the topic of toxic workplaces, I had a fellow panelist comment that she struggled with an anchor client who would berate her for spelling mistakes in her email, in front of her direct manager and because the relationship was a symbiotic one, she was afraid to speak up, let alone clarify why she took that approach to giving feedback. Some people simply abuse power because it is convenient for them to do so. In fact, if the leader isn't aware of their casual comments, it can become a challenge for the direct reports to even bring awareness to it in fear of being verbally abused for doing so. It is also important that you don't form a reputation of being a leader who runs his mouth. Even when it comes to sharing your blunt opinions, even if they are personal, it creates an impression on everyone who gets to hear it. If the opinions that you share to your direct reports publicly lack substance, it reflects badly on you as the leader. And even in the case where you do have a point, the way you put it across also comes under scrutiny. The question to ask yourself if this has been your style, is to see if you would like a taste of your own medicine. Would you be open to receiving feedback from others in the same, exact manner? If yes, why and if no, why? Giving the answers to this question as a way of forming the context allows others to understand how you operate and why you do it this way.

Passive Aggressive Behaviour

This is the type of feedback where a leader thinks, *'This work lacks quality'* but doesn't say a word about it verbally. Instead, they simply start micro-managing their direct report a lot more. They start zoning in on you and the work you produce to ensure you are on the right track. They don't openly say what is wrong, but their behaviours clearly indicate that they have a concern with the work that is being produced. Once I had a client who was excluded from a project that she was supposed to be a part of. It was a move that was unannounced and came as a shock when she found out. Upon confronting her manager about it, she realized that her manager had a lot of concerns with regards to her work which she hadn't openly shared with her. At the end of the meeting, my client merely asked her manager, 'If you had so many concerns with my work, why didn't you mention anything back then? Why didn't you say something?' Her manager was at a loss for words and it was pretty clear that both parties needed to have more open conversations in order to work effectively as a team. Taking the passive-aggressive route only serves to backfire on leaders because they didn't set expectations properly and give feedback that inspires their team members. Behaviour changes are hard for people to read, especially if they are new or not yet tuned in to your personality and leadership style. Many times, it can be hard for your direct report to uncover the real reason behind your behaviour change and might lead to assumptions. Every leader has their set of quirks that may or may not be conscious to them so it helps to check-in with your direct reports to know if they need any clarifications on the instructions you have given them.

Blunt Actions

Some leaders take it to the extreme by standing behind the individual's chair to ensure they are completing the work they were assigned. One of my coaches mentioned a harrowing experience where her boss embarrassed her in front of all her colleagues. Not only did she stand there with her hands on her hips, standing behind and staring down at her, she even made rude comments on the work that was being produced, since my coach was rushing to finish a report that was overdue.

Behaviours like these make the individual look bad and are embarrassing for everyone on the team. However, there are leaders who resort to such blunt actions without thinking about the consequences. It could be because they were subjected to the same kinds of behaviours as a new employee and they do not know how to give feedback that inspires. Some leaders take the workload from a particular individual and pile it on someone else who is known to produce better quality work. All of these are blunt actions that leaders take to send the message across in a toxic manner. Truth of the matter is, not all leaders are good leaders. Some just enjoy being jerks.

Giving feedback can be a challenge to many. Some have the natural skill to communicate effectively on topics that are sensitive. They may be more emotionally intelligent and are better at reading the cues of the other party's body language. Humans care a great deal about being liked and tend to think highly of themselves. Our brains are wired to react more strongly to negative feedback as opposed to positive ones. So it is not unusual to see leaders claim to be a good manager but dread to give feedback when required. Employees also dread receiving critical feedback because of the way it makes them feel internally. As a result, there is a bias amongst both parties to navigate towards what we want to hear instead of what needs to be heard. Giving feedback and receiving it is an equally hard process, but once you master the skill of giving and receiving with grace, using candor, you are well on your way to become a much better leader.

According to Kim Scott, author of *Radical Candor*, it is all about building strong relationships with the people you work with.

Developing trust is not merely about completing work in a reliable manner. It goes deeper than that. Kim postulates that developing candor consists of two dimensions; 'caring personally' and 'challenge directly'. Caring personally means you need to see the human side of the person you are working with instead of looking at them like a machine who is paid to do the work you assign them. It is about being more human, caring for the person, and sharing more than who you are at work. The older generation grew up with the notion that work and personal life should be kept separate at all times. Many leaders still practice this today and have strong boundaries over what they are willing to converse about aside from work related topics. To have a good relationship, you have to be your true self and share all of your other identities that you carry aside from being a boss. You can be a mother, a sister, wife and daughter on top of being the leader of your team. You also carry the identity of being someone who loves sports, baking or traveling. All of these identities belong to you, and sharing a little bit about who you are and what makes you, you aren't going to destroy the working relationship you have with your colleagues.

The other aspect she talks about is challenge directly. Let's say you are in a team meeting and someone within your team says a comment like, 'All women are really bad drivers' or they could say to a female colleague, 'Hey, women are known to be great at taking notes. Can you make sure you take all the meeting notes and at the end of the meeting, share the minutes with us?', even if the person who said that is at the same peer level. A very simple strategy to deal with such comments which are non-confrontational, doesn't hurt the relationship and is very safe in Asian workplaces, is to simply repeat the same exact phrases they mentioned after them. For instance, 'So what you're saying is, all women are bad drivers?' Repeat the exact phrase they said back to them and get them to clarify what they said by ending the question with a pause. Same for the other example, 'So you're saying that she can take good notes and everybody else wouldn't?' All you are doing in such situations is heightening the awareness levels of the individual's bias in a safe, non-confrontational way by displaying curiosity. The energy in which you communicate this should be one of curiosity, not sarcasm. Now, just because you reflected their statements, it does not mean they might have a proper response to it. It's not realistic to expect any response in such situations. However, what you have done in this scenario is to get them to be aware of their unconscious biases as well as provide them with the opportunity to think twice before making such statements at the workplace. It can be difficult to come up with the right words when such situations occur, so this technique of 'parroting' their statements and asking it back as a question helps you to practice candour effectively.

Telling people their work is not good enough comes with the territory of being a leader. The key is to avoid the extremes of naming them and shaming them for their shoddy work or taking a passive aggressive approach by pushing them over to another manager because you cannot give them the feedback they require to become competent. Telling people they are not going to get the promotion they wanted because they are lacking in several areas is hard. Making hard calls on who does what on the team is hard. Keeping high standards for the quality of work and rejecting anything that is sub-par is hard. But most leaders struggle with communicating these things even if they have the right intentions. Criticizing people and their work can seem like a bad way to build a relationship but once your team members know that you really care, it can make a world of difference to the performance you get from them. Having candor allows you to build trust and opens the door for the kind of communication that gets you the results you are aiming for. Once people trust you and believe you care about them, they are much more willing to take your feedback seriously and act on it. They also become more willing to give you feedback on what you are doing well and what you could improve on. So many of us are conditioned to sugarcoat our words or not say what needs to be said because we don't want to hurt anyone's feelings. This is an adaptive behaviour that helps us avoid conflict but at the same time, can turn out to be disastrous in a working environment where everyone needs to bring their A-game. When feedback is done right, your team members will start to feel grateful to know that their boss has got their back. They become grateful for the fact that someone on their team cares enough to tell them the truth as it is. That doesn't mean that they won't feel any emotions while receiving the feedback. It simply means they will take some time to digest what has been said, but they will take the feedback seriously and put in effort to make real behavioural change in a sustainable manner. When candor is encouraged within the team, communication flows easily and resentments get resolved as they bubble to the surface. People not only start loving the work they do but also where they work and whom they work for.

New Data, New Decisions

Many times, people are afraid to make changes if they have already decided on one method of working. They worry that changing directions might affect the way their team looks up to them. However, this couldn't be further away from the truth. We have to get comfortable with being agile. With new data, you are able to make new decisions. The new data warrants that. It is proof that you know better with the data you have and it is wiser to make amends and correct course immediately instead of waiting for things to come to a nasty end. However, the data you bring in must be good and it must be presented well for people to want to take action on it. According to Chip Heath and Karla Starr, authors of *Making Numbers Count*, data needs to be communicated properly for people to be moved to take action. Imagine this:

Summer and Bella work for a fast preparation restaurant. They have data on their customers and they are presenting it to their bosses. They stand in the room and say,

> Our typical customer is thirty-two years old, married. Ninety-three per cent of them do full time work and a typical customer on an average has two children. The reason why they buy our product is because of convenience, familiar flavor and nutritionally not as bad as our competitors.

Did you get a clear picture from the data they presented to their bosses? How about if we switch it up and make some changes?

A typical customer is thirty-two years old. Finishes work by 6 p.m., and then picks up her two kids from daycare—two-year-old and a four-year-old—and drags them to the supermarket along with her because that's where she is picking up our product. When she's trying to get the product off the shelf, the four-year-old is creating a ruckus around the supermarket. She finally has the product in her hand and when she's trying to read the nutritional information, her two-year-old child keeps banging on it. Based on this, we suggest that we make the nutritional information and the familiar flavor fonts bigger on the packaging because these reasons are mainly why they buy our product.

This makes a lot of sense because the data was presented properly. The same level of detail is required when we want to speak with candor in order to move people to take action with the new data that is presented to them.

Getting Started on Candour

When you think about developing a culture of using feedback to better one another, people might have their reservations about it. It might seem like a good idea but putting it into place might still seem like a faraway goal. The way to get around this feeling is to explain what it means to have candor, and then asking people to get really candid with you. Show them that you can handle the feedback before you even start to dish out feedback. And when you start giving feedback, make sure you start with praise, make it really specific before you move on to criticism. Getting people to critique you is the best way to be a role model. It also helps to prove that you are also aware of times when you are in the wrong and you would like to be informed about it. Your people should not fear to challenge you when they think you are wrong. Once you get to this stage, you will have a steep learning curve from the very people who report to you. The moment they experience psychological safety with you, they can be open and candid with the feedback they have for you. It could save you a lot of trouble and prevent you from making any costly mistakes. Most importantly, you will learn what it feels like to be on the receiving end of feedback and criticism. The perks of knowing this is, you get better at delivering feedback as a leader. You will have a better idea how your feedback lands with others and improve your ability to build trust in your working relationships. In your pursuit of establishing candor with your team, be careful of critiquing the criticism your team delivers. If you observe someone critiquing a colleague inappropriately, make them aware of it. If someone critiques you inappropriately, listen with intent and reward the candor. The best way to build trust and respect within your team and organization is to show that you can listen to criticism and react well to it.

CEO of Gilt Groupe, Michelle Peluso, says that showcasing where she is good at, where she's not doing so well, and highlighting where she needs help has allowed her teammates to feel safe to do the same. Getting people comfortable in criticizing you takes some time and effort, so be sure to get started on this on a one-on-one level before you bring it to a public level. Getting people used to a culture of candor will require some structures on your end to ensure everyone experiences the psychological safety that you are building with them. People will be reluctant at first, but when you encourage them to criticize you publicly, you earn their trust and give them the chance to open up. It also highlights your willingness to be criticized. It also sets the tone for the team to be willing to embrace criticism in person and in public to do their jobs better. Too many leaders fear that such exercises will undermine their authority as a leader. We have always been taught to suppress dissent but as a 5G Millennial leader, showing a good reaction to public criticism can be the best thing that establishes your credibility as an authentic leader. The easiest question you can ask them to give you criticism is, 'What are some things that I should start, stop or continue so that it becomes easier for you to work with me?' This question should start things rolling.

Of course, you have to expect people to deflect and avoid the question in the initial phase as they become comfortable in critiquing their boss. Most are likely to say they don't have anything on their minds because they don't want to get into any trouble for saying what is really on their mind. They hope to change topics because this is an uncomfortable one. It is even possible that their discomfort can make you feel uncomfortable. This is where you have to be warm yet assertive. You have to prepare for these scenarios in advance and commit to sticking with the conversation until you get a genuine response. The way you can stick with the conversation is to count to ten in your head slowly. Make your team or colleague feel the silence and let it drive them into taking action. Make it harder for the person to stay silent as opposed to giving you genuine feedback. If they clam up in this situation, after trying all of the above techniques, rearrange another time for this to continue.

Once people have started opening up, you have to reward their behaviour by showing you really did welcome their feedback. If you agree with the points they made, make a change as soon as possible. Do something obvious to show that you are trying. It is important for the other party to know that their criticism sent a strong signal and there was a follow up based on their points. Even something as small as catching them when they do the right things can go a long way to help those who give feedback feel heard. In the instance you disagree with the criticism they brought forward, find something in the criticism that you agree with. Even if you might not fully agree with their points, there may be elements of it that you do. Ask them for clarification on the points that they have raised to ensure you understood what they said properly. Then give yourself some time to think about their points and let them know you will get back to them after letting this criticism stew in your mind for a bit. When you say you will get back to them, make sure you schedule a time in your calendar to show that you will. If change is not possible, giving an honest explanation of why it is not possible is the next best option to showcase candor. Micheal Dearing of Harrison Metal used a simple technique to ensure people gave him candid feedback and felt comfortable in challenging him. He put an orange box with a slit on the top in a high traffic area in his office where people could drop questions and feedback. Then, during the Q&A sessions, he answered the questions and cleared the feedback on the cuff. By proving that he would fix problems while embracing feedback, he created a culture of candor within his organization. Eventually, people found it easier to ask him questions in person instead of using the orange box to get their criticism across.

When it comes to giving feedback and having difficult conversations, we usually assume this has to be a timely affair that involves emotionally charged exchanges. This couldn't be further from the truth. Being candid with someone can happen spontaneously, in between meetings, during lunch conversations or while taking a walk to the bus stop after work. Most leaders assume that giving feedback has to be a timely affair and keep it off for later. The problem with such an approach is that the recipient forgets the context in which you wanted to deliver the feedback as the time flies. It makes it hard for you to give specific feedback that will actually be of help. It is important for leaders to be clear when they give feedback. Giving it candidly or informally in the moment or as soon as possible makes it easier for both the person who gives and receives the feedback. The longer you hold on to the pointers and wait till the performance review, the less credible your feedback becomes for the other party. Even your memory might do you a disservice if you don't remember the details clearly and cannot offer a clear clarification when the recipient asks for it. Articulating the context and the issue will become harder the longer you delay. The only exception to giving immediate feedback is to ensure you are not caught up in your emotions. Be sure to be in control of your emotional state before you give candid feedback to others in your team.

What to do when You get Triggered?

A quick technique to practice is the 'SBNRR' sequence.

1. Stop whatever you are working on. Don't react; pause.
2. Breathe in deeply. It takes at least six seconds to process an emotion.
3. Notice the thoughts, feelings, and bodily reactions happening within you. Force yourself to notice and if possible, write down answers to the following questions:
   a. What am I thinking?
   b. What am I feeling?
   c. What sensations can I notice in my body (i.e. jaw clenching, fist clenching, etc.)?
4. Reflect upon whatever you are noticing. What are the facts and what is the narrative I am telling myself? What are the truths in this situation? What options do I have?

Respond to the trigger once you have calmed down. What is the conscious action you choose to take as a response? How do you want to show up as the best and highest version of you? Then choose a wise response.

The way to get people to open up to you and have honest, candid conversations on how we can be continuously improving is to focus on the core principles of caring personally and challenging directly. Practice managing the different triggers that evoke strong reactions from you and be a role model to your team. This is not a skill you save for a performance review type of event, but rather something you give on a regular basis and accept from your team. Candid responses are usually taken more seriously and tend to be more accurate when it comes from someone who spends a considerable amount of time with you at work. As long as you are implementing these two key principles while communicating with candor, you're good to go.

Think about it

Questions to practice candor with your team before meetings/projects/presentations:

- What would make this a success for us?
- What's the one thing you would like to see me start doing?
- What's the one thing you would like to see me stop doing that would be helpful to the team?
- Is there something that I have missed or am not doing that would make this even better?

Questions to practice candor with your team after meetings/projects/presentations:

- How can we change our meetings to be even more effective?
- On a scale of 1–10, how successful did you think this project was?
- What are the reasons/pointers that support the number you arrived at?
- What would we need to do to make it to a 10?

Chapter 8: Coping Mechanisms: Dealing with Stress, Burnout and Overwhelm in Times of Uncertainty

One is not stressful because of what they are doing; one is stressful because he is a bad manager of himself. It is not the nature of the job which makes one stressful.

—Sadhguru

Reading this quote made me stressed out as I started thinking if I was completely losing control of myself. The very thought that it was not my job that was stressing me out, but rather my inability to manage everything that is going on around me made me wonder, how does one do it? How do you manage it all and that too, effectively? It started with my thoughts that never stopped, even at night. My head was buzzing with so many thoughts even as I lay down on my bed, desperately trying to sleep. My sleep cycle was wrecked, and every day I had a voice asking me the same question, *'Will I be able to sleep properly tonight?'* The constant buzz of thoughts that kept circling in my head didn't help me relax. Even exercise didn't help. I would just end up more tired and unable to sleep. I felt drained, physically and emotionally. Even the breaks I took felt useless. My energy levels stagnated despite my breaks. My passion for the work I did was dwindling, I knew something was off, but I just couldn't put my finger on it. I felt like a zombie, and it puzzled me. The work that I did was something that really kept me going. I was passionate about it. I enjoyed the work I did. It brought me meaning and fulfillment. Yet, the constant emotion I felt within myself was best described, for lack of a better word, as 'meh'. Then, sometime in 2021, Adam Grant released an article that piqued my attention. There was a name for the 'meh' I was experiencing. It is called languishing.

It's known as the neglected middle child in mental health. It wasn't a burnout because I could still go on. I had energy. And it wasn't depression either because I didn't feel hopeless. It was a mix of being joyless and aimless. It consisted of a pattern of putting my head down and continuing the grind. There was nothing exciting to look forward to. According to Adam Grant, languishing is a sense of stagnation and emptiness. It dulls your motivation and focus and was described as the dominant emotion of 2021. Many of us were hit with something that we had never quite experienced before. Something that stretched our hopes thin as the pandemic continued with no clear end in sight.

In psychology, we look at mental health on a spectrum of depression to flourishing. Flourishing is known as the peak of well-being. You know what you are up to, you are happy, you are fulfilled, you have purpose and you feel you have achieved a sense of mastery over most areas of your life. Depression is the valley of ill-being; you feel drained, tired, and even your efforts to rest don't help you raise your energy and excitement levels. Languishing is the kind of emotion where you feel the void between depression and flourishing. In other words, it is seen as the absence of well-being. You're not showcasing any symptoms of mental health issues and yet, you're not exactly your normal self either. In terms of productivity, you're not at your 100 per cent. The bottom half of your to-do list keeps recycling itself from one week to the next, making you wonder why some things are just so hard to get done.

Initially, I thought it was all because of COVID. It tampered with our plans, put us on a roller-coaster ride of lockdowns and restrictions and made us uncertain of the future. By April 2020, 2.6 billion people had gone into lockdown and places of employment for 81 per cent of the global workforce were fully or partially closed. A huge percentage of knowledge workers began doing their jobs from home, collaborating on Zoom, whose daily active users skyrocketed from 10 million to 200 million. This sudden shift did what very few have been able to accomplish before; expose how thinly stretched and worn down we all were.[37]

But after diving deeper into this topic, I started to realize that the issues I faced, and many other Millennials like myself, started way before the pandemic even began. It's not like these tasks were high priority items that needed to be ticked off the list asap. They were just the daily chores of everyday life. Simple tasks like folding the clothes at home, paying the bills, sending the microwave oven for repair, responding to text messages from old friends wanting to catch up, bringing my pet for a checkup and many others like these. Anne Helen Peterson, author of the book *Can't Even*, calls this cycle 'errand paralysis'. Something minor gets on the to-do list and it sits there week after week after week. 'Adulting'—the word that has been adopted to describe the fear of doing or pride in completing tasks associated with our parents—has been transformed into a verb. The modern Millennial is seen to view adulting as a series of actions as opposed to a state of being. Living in the modern world is both easier and yet unfathomably complicated. Our mental energy gets allocated to a number of tasks that require our best—which usually is where work tasks come in. By the time we get to the personal tasks that stare at us back home, our energy is depleted for the day. What's worse, is that we feel a sense of shame for not being able to have the energy to do these small things right.

> *'The pandemic has had a tremendous impact on my well-being—I've had mental health challenges, and I've hit major roadblocks with that. My physical health has changed because I can't exercise like I used to. It's affected me economically. I feel like my career has been set back again.'*
>
> —Amelia Tan, Millennial

---

[37] Moss, J. 2021. *The Burnout Epidemic: The Rise of Chronic Stress and How We Can Fix It.* Harvard Business Review Press.

It's not that the small tasks were impossible to do. No. It's just that focusing on those tasks would take away the energy needed to excel at the workplace, and that is not a trade most Millennials are willing to make. This generation is so used to prioritizing energy on activities that advance our career that we inadvertently end up realizing that we are on the road to burnout. Covid just accelerated the process for us. According to many individuals, the pandemic weighed heavily on the workers but employers still asked their people to engage in work as usual. Expectations on deadlines still seemed to pressure leaders to get their team members to work as if they didn't have any issue. In fact, for many, the mental wellness activities felt like an extra activity to complete instead of serving as a tool that helps them cope with burnout.

'It's ironic. They've introduced an app for me to calm down but shouldn't they be looking into making the workplace less stressful? It all seems a bit tone-deaf.'

—Millennial

Burnout VS Exhaustion

Burnout was first seen as a psychological diagnosis in 1974, by psychologist Herbert Freudenberger, for individuals who collapsed as a result of overwork. The medical community has long argued about how to define burnout. In 2019, the World Health organization (WHO) finally included burnout in its International Classifications of Diseases (ICD-10), describing it as 'a chronic syndrome conceptualized as resulting from chronic workplace stress that has not been successfully managed'. It is characterized by three dimensions:

1. Feeling of energy depletion or exhaustion
2. Increased mental distance from one's job, or feelings of negativism or cynicism related to one's job
3. Reduced professional efficacy

The WHO definition is important because it acknowledges that burnout is more than just an employee problem; it's an *organizational problem* that requires an *organizational solution.* From what I've observed, most leaders know that burnout is an issue, and companies are getting on board to offer services and perks to help employees lower their stress and improve their well-being. However, despite these attempts, burnout is on the rise. This isn't something that happens overnight. It is a slow erosion of coping mechanisms to adapt to the daily chronic stress that finally overwhelms. The current state of matters is a great reminder to Millennial leaders like yourself about what burnout is and what it isn't.

The real reason for this is that we are ignoring the systemic and institutional factors that are the real causes of burnout. If you want to address the burnout problem, the first step is repeating and internalizing this mantra: burnout is about your organization, not your people. Yes, yoga, wellness apps, meditation apps, and vacation time can help people feel optimized and healthier, but it is merely a short-term solution. Suggesting wellness strategies that place ownership on individuals for preventing and managing their own burnout is dangerous.

How Quick-fix Initiatives Backfire

A client I was working with shared with me his struggle with burnout. The place he was working with had wellness initiatives which had Pilates programs on Tuesdays and no zoom meetings on Fridays. All of these were well intentioned initiatives but it didn't help my client. When he was drowning in work, it was hard for him to walk past his colleagues with a yoga mat under his arms to go to the Pilates class. It just didn't feel right to him and he worried about being judged for using such initiatives when he was behind on work. The thought of spending time on these activities felt like a guilt-trip to him. When you're burnt out and overworked, it is very difficult to see these initiatives as valuable. My client couldn't see himself going out to do pilates because he felt like he would be looked at as someone who has too much work on his plate and yet is heading off to a Pilates class—which is non-work related. So such benefits are often resented by those who are going through burnout because they cannot enjoy them despite them being there. Burnout shuts participation and the ability to relax, especially when you are around your boss and colleagues. If you're feeling burnt out and stressed with trying to get work done with looming deadlines, the last thing you feel like doing is going to a Pilates class to become more mindful.

The irony of it all? According to many HR professionals, the people who participate heavily in such wellness initiatives are the ones who are the least burnt out and stressed out. It's the teams that aren't under any pressure that really participate in such activities. To top it off, the wellness programs get really great reviews from people who don't really need it and management takes that feedback and introduces more initiatives like these and wonder why the people who feel burnt out aren't being more productive. It's easy to provide a well-being toolkit of courses and programs, but what's harder, and much more required of leaders, is to step into the mess and realize the issues on the ground and tailor customized initiatives to overcome the problems.

We need to look at ourselves as leaders, at the role our organizations play, and use our voice to tackle this monster. We need to step into the complexity of the problems that people in our team encounter and be the voice for the people on the ground.

Here's an email that I co-wrote together with another mentee who was struggling to speak up about building stronger boundaries with her boss. With most teams working from home, workers were expected to work beyond the typical working hours and my mentee was struggling with her boss who expected her to reply to emails within the hour— even on weekends! Such unexplained expectations are unhealthy and it is important to communicate the same in a soft yet assertive manner.

> Boss,
>
> I appreciate that you are passionate about work and detail focused. However, when I receive emails on the weekend, it interrupts my ability to rest and have mental downtime. For my own mental health, I need you to respect my need for rest. If I receive an email on the weekends, please know that I will not read it unless the subject title says 'Urgent'. If I receive emails on weekends regularly, I will not be able to maintain my energy levels during the week and this will impact my morale and productivity.
>
> I hope you can support me on this in the future.

If you are facing an issue from your own boss, be the leader that you need and speak up. It can make the difference and your own team will appreciate the fact that you are walking the talk. Withholding feedback is choosing comfort over growth. Staying silent deprives people of the opportunity to learn. If you are worried about hurting feelings, it is a sign that you haven't earned enough trust in that relationship. In healthy relationships, honesty is an expression of care.

Although developing emotional intelligence skills like optimism, gratitude, and hope can give people the fuel they need to be successful, If an employee is experiencing burnout, it is the leader's responsibility to stop and ask why. What we commonly see is that wherever we see a problem, we need to blame someone for the problem. But most of the problems that we see are not because of individuals. They are because of systemic issues. Issues that arise from how the system is designed. There is no point in blaming a crash on a sleepy pilot but it is important to ask why was this pilot sleepy if this is a repeating behaviour? In Singapore, the recent news has been about young doctors working for twenty hours and feeling exhausted. At the nineteenth hour, when the doctor is writing the prescription and calculating the dosage, if he or she makes the mistake, it is a systemic issue. If you, the leader, cannot get the desired outcome or the performance you are looking for again and again and find yourself falling victim to a certain situation, check the system. Don't even blame yourself or the people under you. Suggesting the idea of practicing more grit, joining new yoga classes or downloading a mindfulness app will not help them in the long term. It doesn't help to prevent or cure burnout; it merely helps one to feel good in the moment. A good culture is like a well-executed recipe. Having the right people, the right policies, and the right leadership is key to prevent your people from suffering burnout. Likewise, when you have a bad culture, it merely means that these components are not combining properly. When it comes to burnout, culture plays a critical role. Even though our employees are responsible for their own happiness, leaders play a significant role in providing the conditions that support their happiness.

Gallup data indicates that only 15 per cent of the global workforce is engaged at work. We spend roughly 50 per cent of our waking hours at work. When work feels great, we are engaged and energized. It increases our satisfaction levels by giving us meaning and a sense of accomplishment. However, with the level of disengagement seen at the workplace today, it seems like work has taken on a reductionist reputation. Burnout differs from exhaustion, even though they are both related. Exhaustion means you are pushed to a point where you can no longer continue; burnout is reaching that point and pushing yourself to keep going indefinitely. Burnout tends to start with exhaustion, but soon it turns into shame, or doubt, or both about our capabilities. Our feeling of self-efficacy deteriorates and brings on a sense of cynicism and helplessness. When one experiences burnout, they don't experience the joy of completing an exhausting task. It is the sensation of dull exhaustion that doesn't go away with sleep or vacation. You can tell that your head is barely above water and even the slightest mishap, like falling sick, could leave you feeling permanently damaged. Increasingly, burnout turns out to be more of a contemporary condition as opposed to a temporary one. This shouldn't come as a surprise, as authors of the book *One Second Ahead*—Rasmus Hougaard, Jacqueline Carter, Gilian Coutts—say we are in what they call a 'PAID reality'.

P - Pressure
A - Always On
I - Information Overload
D - Distracted

As a result of the drawn-out pandemic, paid reality we live in and the low attention spans of our minds, we are in a constant struggle to manage the internal mess that is constantly brewing. Even if the pandemic may eventually phase out, leaders have to realize the importance of being able to manage ourselves in such situations. We have been constantly adapting to these new circumstances and getting better at it one step at a time. When we first experienced lockdown, wherever you were, you went through a period of disorientation. You didn't know how to really work from home. You didn't realize what you needed to ensure you have a pleasant working experience. But over time, as you got oriented, you started looking into buying better cameras, fixing the lighting, soundproofing your rooms and buying better gadgets to enhance working from home. Even if it might have taken you some time to do so, the best thing is you were able to improve over time. The same concept applies for our mental states. Initially, we experienced chaos, and as the pandemic dragged out, we realized that our mental state is in a limbo. Now, we have to take up the responsibility to find out how we can better manage our emotions. This is where mindfulness comes in. Simply put, mindfulness is trained attention. It is about being in control of the spotlight and shining it where it is required. If you are at home and worrying about work in your personal time, your mind is not in your control. If you are working and your thoughts are drifting towards personal matters, your mind is not in your control. The ability to control your mind comes—like anything else—from practice. Mindfulness techniques enable people to manage their attention, improve their awareness, and sharpen their focus and clarity. Victor Frankl, who survived a Nazi concentration camp, wrote, 'Between stimulus and response there is a space. In that space is our power to choose our response. In our response lies our growth and freedom'.

Despite his extreme conditions, he managed to choose his response rather than be a victim of his own reactivity. You can easily be one of the people who is going through burnout or has already burned out. This is where you need to learn the best ways to cope with your current experience. You have to go through the process of understanding what burnout really is and what it truly means to live in a world with a burnout epidemic happening all around us. Once we understand this phenomenon better, we are better placed as leaders to identify the role we can play in stopping the spread of burnout. According to leading experts on burnout, Christina Maslach, Susan Jackson and Michael Leiter, here are the main causes of burnout.

Overwhelming Workload

The legacy of overwork has been a problem for ages. The International Labor Organization reports that excessively long working hours contribute to the deaths of 2.8 million workers every year. Work related pressure has increased over the years with more than one-third respondents citing excessive workloads and tight deadlines as their biggest concerns. Add a pandemic to the mix and we can literally understand the meaning of the phrase, 'The shit has hit the fan'. The pandemic acted as an accelerant to an already-overworked society which made for an alarming increase in burnout in 2020. According to data from NordVPN, which tracks when users connect and disconnect from its service, the United States added three more hours to its workday, while France, Spain and the UK stretched theirs by an additional two hours. One person said,

> 'It seems like everyone in my company and my team is working more intensely and longer each day. It's a period of very concentrated effort, which does not feel sustainable. Working remotely is adding more stress, by requiring more calls to align/check-in/work together. In addition to that, the workload seems to be increasing, and as we are absorbing/delivering more, it seems we are also getting asked to do increasingly more.'

As workdays lengthened and meetings increased, most of us were still feeling mentally foggy, stressed about countless outside factors, including our physical health and safety. A global study of more than twelve thousand employees, managers, HR leaders, and C-suite executives across eleven countries discovered that during the stress of 2020, forty-two respondents still felt pressure to meet performance standards, 41 per cent said they were expected to handle more routine and tedious tasks, and 41 per cent said they were juggling unmanageable workloads. What if you are struggling as a leader to balance your workload? Take relief in knowing that you are not alone. As a good leader, you have to walk the walk and continue being a high performer and role model.

In Malcolm Gladwell's book *Blink*, he shares the story of the chair company Herman Miller that engaged Bill Stumpf to design their chairs. In the chair industry, Bill Stumpf is a celebrity and back in the 1980s, he had designed two very successful chairs for Herman Miller— the Ergonomic chair and the Equa chair. This time, they went back to Bill and asked him to design the best possible office chair and to start from scratch. Bill started to look at different data points and he noticed that most of the existing chairs at any office are just one piece. However, in the human body, our lower back and upper back have different needs and hence, they should be two separate pieces. He came up with a prototype and presented it to Herman Miller and they loved it. However, they wanted to market research it. They took some sample chairs to their customers and asked them what they thought.

In the world of chairs, there are mainly two things that companies ask about. The first data point is collected on comfort. On a scale of 1 to 10, how comfortable is the chair? The second data point they collect on is aesthetics. How does the chair look to you? After collecting their results, they took a look at what it had to say. The first data point was brilliant. In the world of chairs, getting a 7 out of a 10 was considered really good. This chair model got 8s and 9s and even some 10s. However, for the second data point, they felt like they got a slap on their faces. The chair didn't look that fancy for many. Some said, 'What is this ugly thing? It looks like lawn furniture!' Others said, 'This looks like a Robocop.' Someone even said, 'This looks like the skeleton of a giant antique insect of sorts.' The feedback for the aesthetics was really poor. Herman Miller was in a difficult position. We too often find ourselves in such dilemmas, where we think something is great but the feedback we get is actually not. When Herman Miller conducted this market research, they literally just took the chair and gave people an opportunity to look at it, sit on it, and give their feedback. It was a very quick process and this is the normal market practice. After some deliberation, Herman Miller decided to put out the product because they loved it.

As expected, it didn't do very well for a while. But then, slowly, some designer started to purchase it, it won an award in France, and then it started to appear in TV commercials. This started bringing the sales up by twenty to thirty per cent and it became the best chair in the whole world. The chair I'm talking about here is the Aeron chair. In this story, there are two data points that people were collecting feedback on. Comfort; in a short period of time, by sitting on a chair, you are able to figure out to a great degree if the chair is comfortable or not. However, the second point is really a snap judgment. How the chair looks to you. Because the question was asked, people gave their answer.

It was a quick answer. In our world, we are required to do things that require thought design analysis quickly, almost always, you can't do them properly. There are some things that you can do quickly such as pulling out reports from Salesforce. However, a task like 'Create this PowerPoint presentation for me' is to require thought, design, and analysis. There is no such thing as a quick and proper PowerPoint.

What is the takeaway from this story? When instructions from the top come as 'Do this quickly', it is your role as the leader to look at it and analyze. 'Does this thing require thought, design, or analysis?' If the answer is yes, it is your responsibility to turn around and say, 'If we do it quickly, it won't be properly.'

While everything has changed, expectations that remain the same tend to add a lot of stress even for leaders. The first step is to cut the guilt. As leaders, we are so prone to burnout. We often feel the pressure to move constantly at breakneck speed. We fail to recognize the signs that tell us to slow down. Yet, if you can't protect yourself from burning out, it is going to be harder for you to protect your team from burning out as well. Business as usual is a myth during significant change. It is bizarre that acknowledgement was lacking during this time frame. People need to weigh in on the human factor. Leaders need to cut themselves some slack, and do the same for their team members and employees. The unrealistic expectations that leaders keep on themselves and their teams is one of the reasons burnout spreads so quickly. What works is actually changing the deliverables. If you really want to help your team ease the pressure they feel, you have to adjust the workload.

Perceived Lack of Control

With the juggling demands of work, the expectations of our leadership team, and the need to maintain productivity, it is not surprising that we can fall into the trap of micromanaging. In a burnout situation, nothing could be worse than to display a lack of empathy from the leader's side. Feeling like you lack autonomy, access to resources, and a say in decisions that directly affect your professional life can take a toll on your well-being. Employees who experience burnout are three times more likely to feel micromanaged, according to Susan and Kevin Collins, authors of *Micromanagement: A Costly Management Style.*

Micromanagement can be advantageous in the short term, but it sets you up for failure in the long term. Micromanagement makes sense when you have new employees who need more hand holding, or to coach underperforming employees to make them more productive. The long-term costs of micromanagement can be pretty steep and can lead to typical symptoms such as low morale, high staff turnover, and reduction of productivity. Even leaders who lean in to micromanaging end up as victims of burnout when they fail to delegate enough tasks effectively. It makes them work overtime. Most importantly, everyone wants to feel trusted and have a sense of control over the things they need to get done at work and it is the leader's job to ensure this.

Lack of Belonging

According to social psychologists, groups that provide us with a sense of place, purpose, and belonging tend to be good for us psychologically. They give us a sense of grounding and imbue our lives with meaning. They make us feel distinctive, special and successful. They enhance our self-worth and self-esteem. The antithesis of this feeling is isolation, loneliness, lack of meaning in our lives, loss of healthy attachments and burnout. Community drives belonging. Belonging and well-being is at the top of Deloitte's Global Human Capital Trends survey as one of the most important human capital issues. Seventy-nine per cent of respondents said that fostering a sense of belonging in the workforce was important to their organization's success in the next twelve to eighteen months, and 93 per cent agreed that a sense of belonging drives organizational performance. Despite all the tools available to us to stay connected in our rapidly expanding global workforce, it feels as if the more we need to belong, the more we are growing apart.

When it comes to burnout, organizations that are leaning towards high performance don't tend to realize that the high performance is coming at the cost of their employee's health. Employees that once relied on social support and psychological safety will suffer from burnout when they realize that these support systems have been abandoned.

It can feel like the employee has been pushed into the shadows and left to thrive on their own when things got tough. Isolation has increased as a result of the explosion of remote work in 2020 and many individuals are finding it difficult to maintain a strong connection with their colleagues while working remotely. This shift has become permanent for many companies and while it has been received positively, people still yearn to have the human interaction that they used to get before the pandemic. This is why we are seeing more hybrid work arrangements where teams come to the office on certain days to work together with their colleagues. Studies by YouGov show that Millennials are the loneliest generation with three in ten always or often feeling lonely. At work, 66 per cent of Millennials found it hard to make friends, compared to 23 per cent of Baby Boomers. Personal connection and a sense of belonging isn't just good for engagement and happiness at work, it is what makes us human.

So . . . Are We Doomed?

If the current situation we are in is highly influenced by factors outside our locus of control, it can lead to a sense of learned helplessness. As shown in the figure below, in the greater scheme of things, there are elements that are outside your control. The best you can do in such situations is to accept and adapt. At a smaller scale, there will be some elements that you can influence directly, and all that needs is some effort on your end. At the smallest scale, there are some elements you can completely control. The techniques that I am going to share with you below will help you to work on the elements that you can directly control to ease your stress levels. Will it prevent you from burnout? I doubt so. Will it help? Yes, it can definitely help you to a certain extent. However, it would be wishful thinking to assume that these techniques are the silver bullet to overcome burnout and exhaustion. Bear in mind, these techniques are only useful when you include it in your daily practice.

It's Not Completely on You

The idea I want to instill in you with regards to the post-pandemic stress and burnout we are facing is not a negative reflection of your ability to manage your stress levels. With the rise of the internet and growth of mobile devices, how and where we work has shifted. The pandemic has allowed us to transition into an alternative that is working well in this situation. Over thousands of years, our brains have evolved to handle a very different kind of work. Humans historically survived through physical labor as hunters, farmers, and even for a period, as industrial workers. During this time, people were self-sufficient and tasks were clear: kill an animal, gather firewood, plow a field. In all these cases, there was a singular focus of work and a clear demarcation between field, forest, factory floor, and home. Today's information-driven work environment is frequently hectic and often ambiguous, with the lines between work and home becoming more and more blurred.

Your Body Stores Stress

Everyone has a stress signature, a certain way that their body feels when they are stressed. Developing an awareness of your stress signature is one of the key ways to relieve your stress. You need to get more acquainted with how and where your body stores its stress can help you uncover the best ways to let go of the tension. As long as the stress remains under the surface of your awareness, it becomes challenging to relax. As you are moving throughout your day, pay attention to your bodily sensations. There are certain areas of the body that are typical 'hotspots' where tension is stored. A common one is the shoulders. Notice how your shoulders feel when you are stressed. If your shoulders are up, you are bracing, that is known as an unconscious response to stress. Practice relaxing your shoulders and allowing them to come down. Check other areas of your body where stress might be stored, such as your stomach, face, neck, chest or back muscles. If they are tense, imagine them relaxing and releasing the tightness. Your body is always listening to you for instructions. Once we get really tuned in to what our body needs, we are able to constantly work on ourselves to remove the stress that has been stored. The stress affects you in three key areas - physically, psychologically and behaviourally. Here are some of the symptoms you might spot when you are under stress:

Physical Symptoms	Psychological Symptoms	Behavioural Symptoms
• Quick heart rate • Shallow breathing • Adrenalin • Muscle tension • Sweating • Digestive issues • Grinding jaw • Tension headaches • Skin disorders • Fatigue • High blood pressure • Change in appearance	• Poor concentration levels • Memory lapses • Emotionally reactive • Moody • Tearful • Depressed • Anxious • Low confidence • Impatience	• Aggression • Withdrawal • Change in eating habits • Poor sleeping habits • Poor time management • Substance abuse • Absenteeism • Low tolerance • Snap easily at others

The Three Levels of Stress

Stress comes in three different levels and they all have very unique characteristics within each type. The key for leaders is to be able to self-diagnose and also be able to identify what kind of stress they may be facing. Only when you are able to diagnose your stress levels properly can you treat it in the appropriate manner. Simply doing a Google search on ways to manage stress will actually prove to be more fatal with a misdiagnosis. The three levels of stress are:

Acute Stress

This is usually brief. If you are late for a really important appointment, you will face acute stress. It is usually brief and is caused by reactive thinking. Some form of event usually causes this level of stress. If a colleague suddenly shouts at you out of the blue, you can experience acute stress. It is usually related to existing or upcoming situations that you are apprehensive of. It can also come from negative thoughts from an argument that are constantly on replay in your head.

Episodic Acute Stress

In this level of stress, life is chaotic and shows indicators of a crisis. When you have many responsibilities and are unable to manage them effectively, you are under episodic acute stress. As the name suggests, you are in a stage where a particular event is causing you stress on a cyclical basis. If you have a toxic boss that likes to pick on you during each and every meeting, it can cause you to be stressed out, especially if the meetings happen every week. Symptoms that indicate you are in this deep are issues of poor organization, inability to meet timelines and deadlines and feeling like you are constantly worrying about something or the other.

Chronic Stress

Chronic stress is the worst of them all, and issues like languishing and burnout fall under chronic stress. It is also the most harmful amongst the three and requires a lot more advanced interventions to cure. Eating healthy and sleeping longer hours and other typical tips might not provide a long-lasting solution to someone who goes through chronic stress. Typically, employees who are facing critical health issues themselves or within their families tend to experience chronic stress levels. Long term poverty, unemployment, dysfunctional family, or unhappy marriage scenarios are also known to cause chronic stress in people.

Stressors You can Manage within Your Locus of Control

#1 Email Addiction

How often do you check your email? A few times a day? Hourly? Every time you see, hear or feel a notification from your phone? Is it even possible for you to go without checking your email for any significant stretch of time? Email dependency is the same as any type of addiction. Whether you receive a thank you message from a client, spam from vendors, or an important email from your boss, your brain releases a neurotransmitter known as dopamine to make you feel good. It creates a craving that lifts your mood and makes you check your email inbox over and over again. Many people leave their email open all day long. You might think it is making you more productive and constantly up to date when you can answer emails shortly upon receiving them. Unless all your emails are urgent and important, you run the risk of being less productive by keeping your email open all the time. If you allow your attention to switch every time a new email arrives, you're wasting time. It takes your brain several seconds to concentrate on a new email, and then the same time again to return your focus to your previous work. It might take even longer if you lose your train of thought. What's worse, is that this shifting of attention back and forth makes you less effective overall.

Being mindful can help you notice this pattern that might be running unconsciously within you. Being mindful puts you in tune with your thoughts, feelings and cravings. When you get the urge to check your email for its own sake, observe it. Before you automatically succumb to the urge, observe it. Take some time out to breathe, slow down and notice what is happening within you. Take back your power to choose what you want to do instead of succumbing to your subconscious cravings. In the first part of the morning, the brain is generally the most alert, focused and creative. Opening your inbox puts you in reactive and firefighting mode. It saps away your early morning creative energy and creates a slow start to your day. Being mindful means you enjoy the start to your day. Keep the first few hours for you to start right. Exercise, meditate, spend some time journaling, listen to your favorite music and enjoy taking a bath. Create a morning routine that gives you joy and prepares you for the challenges ahead. Allocate fixed times during the day to completely focus on emails. These small changes can make a big impact in lowering your stress levels.

#2 Kill All Notifications

Having your emails always on, even if it is only in the background, can create a lot of unnecessary 'noise' both in the lives of individuals and within functioning organizations. One of the simplest ways to create more time and improve mental focus is to eliminate unnecessary noise. Do yourself a favor and switch off all your email notifications, pop-up windows, alarms, and ringtones. Doing so will keep your time between designated email sessions clear for other important work. Over the next week, pay attention to what happens to your focus, your productivity, and your well-being when you get distracted by an email notification. Then, experiment working for another week with the notifications switched off. After that, you can make an informed decision that works best for you.

#3 Enhancing Sleep—Catch the Melatonin Wave

A complex mix of neurochemicals in your brain and body determines the quality of your sleep. Especially melatonin. This chemical, when released from your pineal gland inside your brain, makes you relaxed, drowsy and helps you fall asleep. It is a great, organic, and natural drug. If you learn to notice it and go with its flow, you'll enjoy falling asleep and have better quality sleep during the night. The key to catching the melatonin wave is to be mindful of the natural drowsiness and relaxation that occur towards the end of the evening. Maintain this awareness as you inch closer towards your sleeping time. This becomes hard to catch if you are still looking at screens late into the night.

Your smartphone, your tablet, your television or any other screen you may have tend to stand in the way of you catching the melatonin wave. Each of these screens emit high levels of blue light rays. That blue light suppresses your pineal gland which results in a reduced production of melatonin. Before these devices became common, the sun was the only light setting your neurological clock. Today, artificial light threatens to throw that natural rhythm out the window. Screen light kills your sleep and tricks your eyes to believe the sun is still up. Similar to your morning routine, it is good to have an evening routine that sets you up for a good night's sleep. Turn off all screens one hour before you go to sleep. All of them. Once you experience the impact it has on your sleep quality, you will never want to touch any of these devices late at night again!

#3 Perceptual Activities before You Sleep

Too much thinking is yet another enemy of late evening natural relaxation and drowsiness. Conceptual activities like intense conversations, replying to emails, working, or reading can arouse your attention and suppress your natural sleepiness. However, *perceptual* activities like doing the dishes, going for a walk, or listening to music can help you catch the wave of melatonin as it rises. Simply being mindful of changing melatonin levels can help you better go with its flow. I mean, think about it. Do you have an evening routine? Do you work on your laptop right up until bedtime, even if there is no concrete reason for you to do so? Just a small adjustment to your evening routine can go a long way toward enabling you to prepare for bed with a calmer mind that's more in tune with the natural rhythms of the body.

Are You Stuck with Self-sabotage?

While I have shared with you the practical ways to deal with stress, burnout and overwhelm, it is important to stress that sometimes, it is us who end up self-sabotaging ourselves. I know, it's hard to believe, but yes, there is a possibility that you are the cause of your own distress.

Derek Sivers, founder of CD Baby, mentions this story when he used to live in Santa Monica, California, just right off the beach. He used to cycle down a path of 7.5 miles and if you went on a round trip, it was 15 miles and during the weekdays, this path was almost always empty. It was the perfect opportunity for Derek to go and do his usual ride. Being the person he is, he had always adopted a 'GO GO GO! Push as hard as you can' kind of red-faced type of bike ride. Thanks to the empty path, he used to ride a few times a week and every time he would finish his bike ride, he would look at the watch and it would be around forty-three minutes on average. As time went by, he started to mentally associate exhaustion with his bike ride and his enthusiasm levels to go on the bike ride started to drop. So he decided one day that he's going to dial back the effort, ride just for joy to see what happens and experience how that feels. When he went on this ride, he really started to enjoy it. He noticed two dolphins, a pelican flew past him, and when he looked up, he felt there was something in his mouth.

He said, 'I can still remember the taste of undigested shellfish' and laughed at the novelty of the experience. But then, he looked at his watch and he couldn't believe what he saw on his watch.

'Forty-five minutes. Really? One ride was leaving me completely exhausted, red-faced, panting and it was forty-three minutes and the one that left me rejuvenated was forty-five minutes?' he thought to himself.

All that *'go-go-go-as-hard-as-you-can-push-harder'* only gave him a 4 per cent boost and he could get 96 per cent of the results by actually enjoying the ride without the push-push-push attitude. This experience became an important learning lesson for him for the rest of his life. He started to really question himself in his projects and the work he did. Did he really need to 'Go-Go-Go' or could he achieve the same results by actually relaxing a little bit? Over time, he made a clear distinction between the 'go-go-go-as-hard-as-you-can-push-harder' mindset as just unnecessary stress and anxiety that accompanied the effort that he was making.

Sometimes, things that we think that are really good for us often become a task and a chore. After a certain point of pushing yourself, adopting the 'go-go-go-as-hard-as-you-can-push-harder' attitude is no longer because it is good for you, it's nice outside, or the path is beautiful. It's because it is something that has come up on your to-do list that you have to get done as quickly as possible. We often get into a routine of things that we end up marching through life with very busy packed days while being as quick and efficient as possible with everything we do. This mindset spreads to the activities we do for health, well-being, time with friends and family. All of those things that really contribute to our happiness levels and well-being get neglected. We fail to slow down in a world that keeps speeding up. This is the thing that you have to take time off to reflect about. Look at some of the daily things that you do from the very beginning of your day, when you get up. We rarely hit pause and say,

Think about it

- Wow, am I really self-sabotaging myself by pushing myself all the way in all the different areas of my life?

- Is this serving me and the people around me well?
- What does your morning typically look like?
- What emotions do you feel before you head off to work?
- Is that routine serving you well?
- Is it possible for you to add a 'pause' in there and think about how you could do some things slightly different, such that you get to enjoy the small moments and appreciate them more? Take a look around you.
- What is your environment doing to help you with that?
- Are there people you can pull into your routines to give it a twist or a new flavour?

Like Derek, could you slow your pace down, or ride in the opposite direction, or measure your performance with a different metric, i.e. how much I enjoyed the ride instead of how long it took me to complete the ride. Perhaps you can walk instead of cycling and see how it makes you feel? Perhaps invite a new friend every day to join you for the walk. You are really achieving the same thing but you are just shifting your perspective slightly. These are the small things you can do to bring about change in an easy manner. Change doesn't have to be hard at all. It's really those small moments where you make those tiny tweaks to your routines that may freshen your experience before you reach a stage of not wanting to do it at all. Hit a pause. Be kinder to yourself. Switch things up a bit, and you'll start noticing your happiness levels go up. You don't need to be the one creating unnecessary stress and anxiety, causing you to feel exhausted. It's just not worth it.

Chapter 9: Culture: Building an Environment That Drives Performance

The culture of any organization is shaped by the worst behaviour the leader is willing to tolerate.

—Gruenter & Whitaker

On 11 March 2011, a 9.0-magnitude earthquake struck off the coast of Tohoku, Japan, and resulted in a catastrophic tsunami. Waves as high as 45 feet were created and they struck off the Fukushima Daiichi Nuclear Power Plant. The waves were so high that they easily leaped over the underside sea walls of the nuclear plant and destroyed emergency generators, the sea water cooling pumps, and the electric wiring system. Without any power, the nuclear reactor got heated up because there was no power to cool them down which then resulted in an explosion, injuring a few people at the power plant. The worst thing that happened was that there were radionuclides that were released into the atmosphere which then meant that a lot of the Japanese people who lived in that area had to leave their homes and area so that they wouldn't get any radiation exposure. They wouldn't know when they can come back because it would take thirty–forty years to clean up the atmosphere.

Now although this earthquake, which was labeled as the 'great east Japanese earthquake' was unpreventable, what happened at Fukushima

Nuclear Plant was totally man made. In other words, it could have been prevented. This was revealed in a report that was generated from an independent investigation that was done in 2012. This was a credible result of 900 hours of interviews, nineteen committee members, nine plant tours, and conversations from three town halls. Many people, through the lead up to this particular catastrophe, had warned that we are just waiting for a disaster to happen and something should be done. In fact, in the year 2006, Katsuhiko Ishibashi, a professor at the Research Center for Urban Safety and Security at Kobe university was appointed as a subcommittee member to revise the national guidelines on the earthquake resistance of the country's nuclear power plants. Ishibashi criticized the government's record for allowing these power plants to be built in areas where there is high seismic activity and the vulnerability of the power plant is high and likelihood for earthquakes to happen was really high.

However, the rest of the members of the committee completely ignored what Ishibashi had to say as they all had ties to these power companies. They completely downplayed what he had to say. Ishibashi didn't give up. He spoke up again by writing an article, 'Why worry? Japan's nuclear plants are at great risk from quake damage.' He mentioned in his article that because of seismic activity and plate tectonics in and around this area where this nuclear power plant is, we are just waiting for an earthquake because these things happen in a pattern and an earthquake is long overdue. He clearly said, 'Unless radical steps are taken now to reduce the vulnerability of nuclear power plants to earthquakes, Japan could experience a true nuclear catastrophe in the near future.' Unfortunately, nobody listened. In fact, Haruki Madarame, a nuclear generator and chairman of Japan's National Safety Commission, during the Fukushima disaster, told the Japanese legislator not to worry about Ishibashi because he is a 'nobody'. What he meant by that was that neither was he from the industry, nor was he from the government. He came from an academic background, so they took an attitude of, 'What does he know?' During this period of time, Japan was in real need to be independent of anybody else for their energy needs. Hence, the push and rush to build these nuclear power plants and have them functioning was really high. Despite Ishibashi's warnings, nobody heard. The lesson we can take from this scenario is the importance of listening to people from different perspectives. So what if Ishibashi was from an academic background? He had something really relevant to say. In order to prevent such catastrophes from happening at the workplace, it is the duty of the leader to create an environment where everyone's voice is heard. Having diverse perspectives and creating a space of psychological safety has to be the prerogative of the leader. If leaders don't create that kind of a safe environment for everyone to feel safe enough to speak up, they will inadvertently lose out in the long run and make room for mishaps to happen. And the more mishaps that happen, the more it ruins the employer brand of the organization.

Reputation Carries More Weight Than Money

Companies all around the world are constantly developing what is being known as an 'Employer Brand' in order to stay competitive and acquire the best talent in the market. Employer Branding has now become an essential element of an organization's strategy to position themselves as an ideal employer. Now, 72 per cent of recruiting leaders around the world would agree that the employer brand has a significant impact on hiring.

According to LinkedIn, a company with a stronger employer brand than its competitors on average see a 43 per cent decrease in the cost per candidate they hire. In fact, if you disregard developing your employer brand, you risk paying over $4000 in salary premium per employee hired. Now if you had 10,000 employees in your organization, you could save as much as $7.6 million in additional wages.

A staggering 78 per cent of people will look into a company's reputation as an employer before applying for a job and 88 per cent of Millennials believe that being part of the right company culture is very important. Forty-seven per cent of active job seekers say company culture is a driving motivator when looking for work. So what forms the culture of an organization? What role do you have in contributing to the company's culture?

When it comes to organizational culture, we talk about how people behave in organizations. This ranges from shared values and beliefs to the way employees interact with each other. A lot of the discussion on culture centers on having a retreat and a meeting with leaders who then come up with the vision, mission, and values for the company. They basically aim to define the culture during the retreat. While all of these activities are helpful to a certain extent, the true culture of any organization or team comes from the shared habits, routines or rituals of that company. If it's not actually a habit amongst everyone, it's not really a part of your culture. It just becomes something that was discussed at a retreat which then transformed into a slogan that is put up around the walls of the office space. If you want to shape the culture of your team, you need to first start with reshaping the habits of your team.

If you want to create a culture of having clear work life boundaries, you need to step up as a leader and role model by ending work early and spending time with family, while encouraging your team to do the same. If you want to create a culture of candor where feedback is given openly, you need to be willing to accept feedback as a leader in the same settings. If you want to create a culture of lifelong learning, you need to show your team members what is the latest course you have been learning and implement it by sharing your learnings to your team on a regular basis. Simple activities like sharing what you learnt from what you read or what you tried out after learning, can help reinforce the culture of learning and curiosity amongst the team. As a leader, you need to identify what habits should run deep within the team. Is it related to practicing candor and giving feedback freely? Or could it be related to the way meetings are run under your leadership? The key is to role model the behaviour you want before expecting others to follow suit.

When you understand how organizational culture works, you can use it for your own benefit and turn indifferent employees into engaged, motivated employees. Successful organizational culture takes your service delivery to the next level, improving the quality of life for both your employees and your customers.

Oftentimes, we discount the influence we have on the people we lead because we think it has a minimal effect. However, when it comes to important decisions such as staying or leaving an organization, we always find ourselves considering the people who we will be leaving. Are you eager to leave the people in the organization, or do you feel the tinge of pain when you think of whom you're going to miss?

In order to build a high-performance team, you need to be the kind of leader people will consider as a big reason for continuing in the organization. People leave managers, not organizations. Ed Catmull, the co-founder of Pixar once said that if you do not give people the freedom to fail, then they end up doing derivative work, not innovative work. If one does not have the freedom to fail, they will look for things that have worked in the past and are good enough, safe-to-adopt practices. This is what he defines as derivative work. It is work that is derived by what worked in the past. Innovative work requires you to have the courage to do something completely new. It means that you provide a safe space for people to create many drafts; you allow for feedback to come from all directions and everything is seen as an iterative process. Only an iterative process can bring about innovation. In order for you to make sure that you and your team do not have a derivative way of working, you have to be in love with drafts and several iterations. Only then can you create a culture of innovation within your team. Your culture sets your expectation for what is 'normal'. Create a culture where your desired behaviour is the normal behaviour and you will create a team of performers. Nothing sustains motivation better than creating a tribe that has a strong sense of belonging. The shared identity that you create with the culture you create will reinforce a better identity amongst everyone in your team. It is this friendship and community that embed a new identity and help behaviours last over the long run.

This book has covered the key competencies you will need to lead in the new normal. The final step in putting it all together is to create a culture that is completely unique to you and your team. The beauty of being a leader comes with your ability to bring out the best in your team. The way to do that is to build an environment where people can thrive. Building an authentic culture starts with building a strong sense of community because people are looking for more than a job— they want to feel connected to the mission and they want a sense of belonging and community.

This begins with communication. When people say in the corporate world, 'You only talk. You do not work', I believe that talking is hard work. Research from Canadian academic on business and management, Henry Mintzberg, says that 78 per cent of the time, what leaders do at work, is talk. In today's knowledge economy, talk is work. If you're getting that wrong 78 per cent of the time, then just imagine your productivity. As a leader, just look at your calendar over a week. If you are somebody who leads people, then surely you will believe that talking is hard work. You owe it to yourself to get it right.

Terry Holland shares a life altering encounter with Jack Welch, the former CEO of General Electric. Back in 1969, when Terry Holland was only thirteen years old, he wanted to make a little bit of pocket money by mowing lawns in his neighborhood. One day, he knocks on the door of this house that he had never mowed the lawn before and Jack Welch walks out. Back then, Jack wasn't the celebrity CEO we know him for today. He was just a middle manager in General Electric at that time. Of course, later on he goes on to becoming the most respected and studied senior executive in the corporate world. In this scenario, Terry Holland says to Jack Welch,

'I'm going around the neighborhood mowing lawns and I'd love to provide this service to you.'

Jack Welch responds, 'Sure, and what are your fees?'

Terry Holland says, 'Well, I don't have a set fee but I let people pay me whatever they feel is right.'

Jack responds to this by asking, 'So you have mowed many lawns, what are people paying you?'

'Three bucks,' Terry replied.

At this point, Jack walks a bit further out of his house and says,

'Alright then, I will pay you four bucks for mowing my lawn but the condition is, it has to be so much better than that.'

Many years later, in an interview, when Terry Holland shares this story, he says, 'When I reflect upon that moment, at the age of thirteen, that was like an invitation for excellence. He was willing to reward me for the excellence I demonstrate. Mowing a lawn is mowing a lawn. A task is a task, and I was doing the task, at the most thinking that I shouldn't make a mistake and get into trouble. But Jack was a leader who was hiring me to show him what I was capable of.'

In the corporate world, we ask our people to do tasks. It is our responsibility as leaders to create a culture of opportunity for them to show excellence and not just position tasks as another task. Of course, you have to be clear about making the distinction on which tasks just require 'getting the task done' and where we truly, truly expect nothing but excellence. That is the invitation you need to give to your people to do the best work possible.

Loving Your People and the True Meaning of Love

Once upon a time, a rabbi came across a young man who was clearly enjoying a dish of fish that he was eating. He went over to the young man and asked, 'Why are you eating that fish?' The young man looked up at the rabbi and said, 'Because I love fish!'

The rabbi responded, 'Oh, you love fish, that's why you caught it with a worm, took it out of the water, killed it and boiled it. Don't tell me you loved the fish. You love yourself and because the fish tastes good to you, therefore, you caught it, took it out of the water, killed it and boiled it and ate it.'

So much of love that we see in the world is 'fish love'.

When a new employee joins an organization, it doesn't mean he loves the organization or the organization loves him. It simply means he saw that this organization is one that could provide for all his needs and likewise, his organization felt the same way about him. This is not love. This is simply each person looking out for their own needs. It is not love for the other. The other person (or organization, in this case) becomes a vehicle for the individual's gratification.

If you want to be known as a great leader, you need to focus on external love. That means you need to focus on what you want to give, not what you want to get. Most people make a serious mistake in thinking that 'you give to those whom you love' when in actual fact, the reality is that 'you love those people to whom you give'. True love is a love of giving, not a love of receiving and it is my sincere wish and hope that you get to truly love your people, so that they can love you back as their favorite leader.

Think about it

1. What do you want the culture of your team to look like?
2. What common habits do you want every member of your team to have?
3. What actionable habits and behaviours will display the values of the organization?
4. What are some of the key habits of high-performance teams that you would like to incorporate into your team?
5. How do you want your employees to describe the team culture to others outside of the team and outside of the organization?

How do you want to be remembered as a leader in your organization?

One Last Thing

We've covered a lot of ground in this book, and as you can see, I'm deeply passionate about this stuff. On your journey of leadership, you will face an immense amount of pressure. Pressure is a fact of life. The people who learn to relish it are the ones who become great leaders. These are the people who take huge strides forward when things are going great and knuckle down and forge ahead in life when the heat is on. Failure is not an option for the 5G leader. Pressure ignites their resolve and sharpens their focus.

If you've come this far, you may well have it in you to thrive under pressure too. If you're serious about your leadership success, then *now is the time to commit and take action.* You must transition from high performance individual to high performance leader. Once you make this fundamental transformation, your career and your life will never be the same again. Having the ability to influence people around you, with their trust and faith in you, is the single greatest skill you can attain. It means you will always be equipped to lead people and be welcomed with open arms wherever you go. When you leave, people follow you in your footsteps. They refer to you when they push for a better working environment.

Throughout this book, you've learned powerful concepts and valuable information that when applied can change the way people respond to you as a leader forever. However, all the information and strategies covered in this book are worthless **if you don't take action.**

New Data, New Decisions

If there's one thing I want to emphasize, it is the importance of taking action. With great power comes great responsibility and likewise, with new data, you are now empowered to take new decisions. You have the ability to change the way you lead based on the areas you want to work on. With the insights you have gleaned from this book, you can start to implement new behaviours to advance your journey as a 5G leader.

I want you to sit down right now and write down your action items for the next thirty days, and for the next three, six, and twelve months. If you don't, something else will grab your attention and you'll be off looking for the next strategy, tactic, or silver bullet to become a better leader. I urge you to put the blinders on and execute the information in this book, and if you do, I can assure you, you will reap the rewards. I've listed all my worksheets, scripts, explainer videos, templates and other cool resources that will help you to get there at https://www.vivekiyyani.com/free

I would love to hear all the powerful ways this book has been beneficial for you as a leader. Please send me the lightbulb moments that helped you think and approach the way you lead differently. Nothing makes me happier than hearing from readers. I collect and study all kinds of stories, small, large, or otherwise, print them out, and store them in a jar for memory's sake. That's how much this means to me. When I get yours, I'll send you back a free gift.

To your success,
Vivek Iyyani

Scan QR code to get your bonus resources

Acknowledgements

The book you're holding (or reading on your screen) is the result of hours of interview conversations, lots of keynote presentations, plenty of research from videos, podcasts, articles and social media posts found online. My heartfelt love and admiration goes to the people listed here who have inspired, challenged, and supported me in this process.

This book wouldn't have been possible if not for the many people who helped me throughout the research and writing phase of this book. Firstly, to my parents who have always encouraged my passionate pursuits of writing and speaking even when it wasn't the popular option to choose back in school. Thank you for believing in me more than I believed in myself. I would like to thank my wife for constantly standing by side throughout the writing process. It is your support and understanding that allowed me to push through for this book. To Thoufic, for embarking on the journey of entrepreneurship with me. Our teatime talks over managing people and the lessons learnt across those conversations have been both entertaining and educational. I would also like to thank all the leaders that I've interviewed for this book. Your feedback and comments and sharing of the issues on the ground amidst the pandemic was crucial for this book to have any weight. Thank you for your valuable time and your valuable insights. Thank you for doing your part to empower the next generation of leaders.